Data Migration Framework

Removing the Tech Debt

Krupesh Desai

Technics Publications
SEDONA, ARIZONA

TECHNICS PUBLICATIONS

115 Linda Vista, Sedona, AZ 86336 USA
https://www.TechnicsPub.com

Edited by Steve Hoberman
Cover design by Lorena Molinari

First Printing 2025

Copyright © 2025 by Krupesh Desai

ISBN, print ed.	9781634627436
ISBN, Kindle ed.	9781634627443
ISBN, PDF ed.	9781634627450

Library of Congress Control Number: 2025935826

To Neet-Vinay.

Contents

Acknowledgments

I dedicate this book to my late parents, Vinay Desai and Neeta Desai, whom I lost during the first wave of COVID-19 in 2020. I wish they could see that their once notorious son has become an author. Thank you for giving me the life mantra: "Aspire and Inspire before you Expire." This book is also dedicated to the millions who lost their loved ones and were directly affected, both personally and professionally, during the COVID-19 pandemic.

I want to thank my wife, Greena, for her immense support and optimal planning of our routine life, which allows me to squeeze in enough time for my side hustles. On the professional front, I owe my career as a data migration specialist to Helen Jordan. I cannot thank her enough for trusting my abilities and providing me with my first data migration opportunity in 2014—an experience that has significantly impacted my professional growth. I want you to know that you are the best manager I have worked with in the last fifteen years. Additionally, I must mention Paul Brown, who was not only my manager but also became a friend and philosopher. He took me to new heights as a Business Intelligence Consultant and instilled in me a strong sense of self-belief and confidence in my abilities. I must acknowledge my friend in need, Tom Wheatley, who was the first to read snippets of my initial draft and encouraged me to finish the book.

My affair with databases began at the start of this century when I first learned FoxPro and Oracle 8i. By the second or third semester of my graduation, I had developed aspirations to become a data professional. I was fortunate to have excellent professors who kept me intrigued in the subject and helped me build a strong foundation—especially Dr. Srividhya Murali and Dharmin Shah.

I also want to express my heartfelt gratitude to my mentor, Richard James Chaderton. His mentorship began at a tech hackathon event in 2017 and has continued ever since. He is solely responsible for the business acumen I have developed over the years. Many have positively influenced my life. However, while riding this wave of gratitude, I would like to acknowledge a few significant ones, namely Sune Visti Petersen, Eric van der Sluis, Donald Hudson, Chris Rutherford, and Vivien Pine, for their contributions to my professional life.

I am grateful to everyone who crossed my path and inspired me. However, I also want to explicitly thank those who tried to paint me as an imposter when it was not me in the room who was pretending to know my job. In hindsight, those experiences inspired me to intensify my research and aim for a book rather than just a shiny whitepaper. During the process of compiling this book, I realized that we always have a choice in how we respond to adverse situations and people. Thank you to everyone who taught me something, consciously or unconsciously.

This book would not have been possible without Steve Hoberman, who gave me the opportunity to become an author. I am deeply grateful to Technics Publications, and I struggle to find words to fully express my appreciation.

Introduction

Every business application today will eventually become a legacy system. Will you be prepared when that time comes? Too many organizations treat legacy system decommissioning as an afterthought—until they are forced into a rushed migration due to outdated technology, compliance risks, or operational failures. When that day comes, the difference between success and chaos boils down to whether you have a plan. Business executives and technology leaders often underestimate how deeply entrenched their legacy systems are—until the moment comes to retire them. This book is your guide to navigating the high-stakes challenge of legacy system decommissioning without falling into the common pitfalls that lead to project failure.

With minimal technical jargon and a conscious attempt to prevent oversimplification, the book is for business executives, project managers, and technical leaders responsible for retiring a business-critical legacy system with successful data migration. Whether you're preparing to retire a legacy system or looking to improve your current strategy, the framework presented below and described in this book will help you to navigate the complex data migration challenges associated with decommissioning a legacy business system in your organization.

Decommissioning refers to the process of retiring or replacing a legacy business system. A lack of strategic planning for data migration poses huge risks with monetary and reputational impacts on the business and the brand, respectively. While we are about to exit the first quarter of the twenty-first century, legacy business systems supporting the core business transactions are pervasive across industries and sectors, creating a 'tech-debt challenge', where outdated technology negates the scope of business process improvements and innovations while retiring the tech-debt brings shivers to executives and decision-makers. This book is my endeavor to shed light on the strategic planning for data migration when retiring a legacy system backed by my research and past experiences from the last decade as a Data Migration Lead and a consultant in retiring clinical and administrative systems in the public healthcare sector of New Zealand.

In the summer of 2014, in the southern hemisphere, I took the leap of faith from a software engineer of database disaster recovery and replication solutions in Auckland to a data migration lead contractor in the public health sector in the South Island of New Zealand, retiring a patient management system operational from 1993. During my naive early days, I believed that migrating data from such a legacy patient management system into a modern regional healthcare system would be a one-off project for me. However, I eventually discovered that tech-debt challenges from critical business systems operational from the late 1980s to the early 2000s are widespread across business and industry verticals, making legacy data migration projects a common phenomenon that eventually kept me engaged with multiple clients after my first successful data migration. What I initially viewed as a simple task evolved into a complex beast with many touchpoints across various business units, upstream and downstream data integrations, and few experts or documentation around. My successes, failures, and surprises in migrating data from legacy systems over the past decade have significantly influenced my professional journey and ultimately inspired me to write a book on this topic.

What mainly led to this book was a constructive conversation with a senior business executive contemplating the 'decommissioning' of a vast asset management system—a process set to unfold over the next three years. Three questions I received as a data migration consultant were simple yet profound:

What proactive measures can I take to ensure a smooth transition of a critical business application with minimized risk?
How can I comprehend the magnitude of this tech-debt challenge and be strategic about its solution?
Can I leverage any framework to understand the problem and its strategic solution?

I realized the dilemma of a project or the program manager tasked to lead the tech-debt challenge and felt compelled to create a white paper on this subject. The more I researched with existing academic and commercial literature on how to strategically plan data migration from legacy systems, the more I saw the necessity for a vendor-agnostic and simple framework with guiding principles to help business executives and technical team leaders navigate the complexities of data migration when decommissioning a business-critical legacy business system such as ERPs (Enterprise Resource Planning systems), CRMs (Customer Relationship Management systems), or HRS (Health Record Systems). Thus, the idea for this book was born when my white paper on this subject kept expanding month after month with more information and simplification. The following pages represent the culmination of real-world experiences of successes and failures over three and a half legacy-data migration projects coupled with years of research on best practices for legacy system decommissioning.

In this book, I endeavored to answer the profound questions above with a comprehensive data migration framework for executives to be proactive through every stage of the data migration process. The data migration framework, introduced in the first chapter, can serve as a roadmap for business and technical leaders from the discovery to the execution of tech-debt retirement. After presenting the framework and the significance of having a data migration plan based on it, each subsequent chapter describes one specific framework component in depth with practical questions for stakeholders to facilitate informed decision-making that is well-documented and communicated as the data migration plan. Following the data migration framework described in this book, you can create a strategic data migration plan that minimizes the risks associated with decommissioning legacy systems.

Chapter 1

Data Migration Framework

Data migration for retiring a legacy system deals with the dilemma of the unknown source and the moving target. Let me explain how. Legacy business systems to be retired are usually operational for more than a decade or two, and less likely to have their first key developers and system matter experts in the team at present. In contrast, up-to-date documentation about the data structure of the legacy system could be minimal, coupled with the organic chaos of upstream and downstream data integrations. Thus, you would deal with many unknowns in the legacy system while the target application is being customized, resulting in changes to the target data structures. Therefore, inadequate planning for legacy data migration can lead to unexpected problems that might cause systems to fail, disturb normal business operations, or create costly mistakes in data accuracy. All of these issues can hurt a company's earnings, reduce customer satisfaction, and lead to difficulties in meeting legal requirements.

Although the internet is loaded with best practices and vendor-specific data migration guidelines, failures that exceed the time, budget, and delivery are common phenomena. During my first data migration project, I came across excellent research conducted in 2017 by Dylan Jones of Data Migration Pro, showing that only 36% of data migration projects kept to the forecasted budget, while only 46% were accomplished on time [1]. Legacy systems would not have been so prevalent if retiring tech debts were painless. BridgeHead, a healthcare data management solution provider, surveyed a sample of U.S. hospital Chief Information Officers (CIOs) in 2022 [2]. The survey revealed that over 50% of respondents were responsible for managing five or more legacy applications. At the same time, data migration was the second most important factor, along with several other factors that emerged in the 2022 research that are preventing hospitals from decommissioning legacy applications, including:

- Difficulty in identifying a compelling alternative (26%)
- Challenges in managing data transfer and migration (21%)
- Financial costs associated with decommissioning (16%)
- Competing priorities that take precedence (16%)
- Limited time available to focus on decommissioning (16%)
- Lack of internal agreement on the process (5%).

The above statistics for the same research might be similar for other industries besides healthcare, as legacy decommissioning poses reputational and operational risks across the industry verticals. With this vibrant nature of the problem spanning multiple stakeholders and business units, executive decision-making about archiving unnecessary legacy data, identifying necessary legacy data for migration, and eventually migrating the legacy data with minimized interruption in business continuity could be daunting. Those smart ones who leave the data migration as the problem to be solved solely by the target system vendor are sitting on a giant risk magnet, waiting for unpleasant surprises.

Statistics from the research shared above clearly indicate that data migration is challenging, and its failure can severely affect budgets and deadlines. I acknowledge that any project failure is the failure of the people, not the technology. If the technology is not good enough, it is a failure of the people behind the decision to bring that technology in the first place. Similarly, if data migration causes significant delays and issues in retiring legacy tech debts, it's a failure of people making ill-informed, misinformed, uninformed decisions about legacy data migration, consciously or unconsciously.

At the conclusion of my research, I created a simple framework that assists stakeholders in making the right decisions about data migration.

A framework is a structured and systematic approach or guide designed to help organize, analyze, and solve a specific type of problem. Frameworks provide a set of principles, concepts, or components that work together to address complex challenges logically and consistently. Simply put, a framework is like a blueprint or toolkit that simplifies complex tasks by breaking them down into organized, manageable, and repeatable steps.

My data migration framework, with ten components elaborated in this book, will empower good decision-making by providing a structured approach to analyzing, evaluating, and executing actions. Each component clubs a set of questions for stakeholders to ferret answers and compiles a data migration plan that facilitates a structured and informed execution of data migration and minimizes the risk of change from decommissioning.

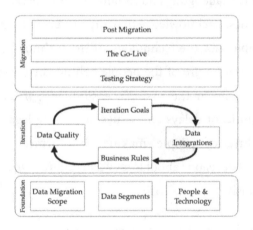

Figure 1: Data Migration Framework

The framework identifies three foundational components (foundation) that further facilitate iterative processes for well-defined test runs (iteration), followed by the last three components that ensure decommissioning with minimized risk (migration). Each component of the framework is allocated a chapter in this book. The "Foundation" phase is crucial as it involves the initial steps needed to align stakeholders and define the scope of the migration project. This foundational work ensures everyone is on the same page and lays the groundwork for a successful transition.

Following this, the "Iteration" phase emphasizes the importance of testing and validating the migration process. During this stage, various scenarios are explored to ensure the migration works as intended before the final implementation occurs. Finally, the "Migration" phase marks the transition where the system is migrated to the new environment, and the old system is decommissioned, completing the overall migration process. Each phase plays a vital role in ensuring a smooth and successful migration.

One or more data migration projects are part of a more extensive retirement project of a business-critical legacy system that usually touches several business units and requires decisions from key stakeholders from business leadership. In some cases, defining the scope of historical data under the migration and building consensus on that scope could become daunting. The complex challenges of legacy data migrations can also highlight gaps and tribal knowledge in your existing data management practices. Higher tech debts with low IT and data maturity could prevent business executives from making informed decisions, introducing significant delays in executing data migration activities.

Considering all the above risk-augmenting scenarios of legacy data migration, I compiled a questionnaire that requests information gathering and decision-making to execute data migration from a legacy system critical for business continuity. These questions and their answers were then re-factored into a plan with the following ten components to minimize the risk of change effectively:

1. Data Migration Scope
2. Data Segments
3. People and Technology
4. Business Rules
5. Data Quality
6. Data Integration
7. Iteration Goals
8. Testing Strategy
9. The Go-Live
10. Post Migration.

The Data Migration Plan

You can bring the proposed framework to action by drafting a data migration plan based on the framework's components. A plan is a proactive artifact containing a set of informed decisions individuals and organizations make to move from Point A to Point B with minimal risks stemming from the change. Retiring a legacy business system can be complex and risky, demanding a thoughtful plan to clear the technology debts with minimal impact on the business continuity.

We need a plan to address, assess, and mitigate risks with thought-through and informed decisions. The ISO 31000:2018 standard for risk management defines risk as "the effect of uncertainty on objectives." When decommissioning a critical legacy system, crafting and following a data migration plan would minimize the risk from the system-wide change.

The core reason for making a plan for data migration is the same as making a plan for your holiday: to assure a good experience and conscious avoidance of unpleasant surprises while doing the actual activity (migration and holiday).

Data migration activity is often overlooked, undercooked, and treated as a technology problem only. The DAMA-DMBOK® also explicitly refers to this ignorance under the data integration and interoperability functional area of data governance. "Data migration projects are frequently under-estimated or under-designed because programmers are instructed to simply move the data; they do not engage in the analysis and design activities required for data integration." [3] Such ignorance of data migration poses a considerable risk, which leads to unexpected results in new business applications, reporting issues, compliance violations, and eventually increasing project costs and delays. Therefore, I recommend crafting a strategy and drafting a plan everyone can agree to follow based on the framework above.

While drafting a plan based on the proposed framework for legacy data migration early in the project, one could anticipate possible risks and challenging situations beforehand. This proactive measure onboards potential stakeholders from various business units and systems to be impacted by the change. I gained first-hand experience creating and executing a data migration plan as a Data Migration Lead in the public healthcare sector. After the successful plan-based data migration project, I worked as an external data migration consultant introduced late in two similar legacy system decommissioning projects in the health sector. Therefore, I was fortunate to witness the chaos and delays in the legacy data migration projects that commenced without plans.

The data migration plan sets the foundation for well-informed and timely decision-making, leading to a coherent solution approach with no surprises on time and cost with the project progression. A legacy data migration attempt without a plan makes decisions on an ad-hoc basis on similar items covered in a planned migration. However, the unplanned approach could face limited time and cost flexibility constraints, leading to chaos, stress, and reputation risk for the executives and the organization.

Have you ever encountered or overheard a situation where a legacy system retirement was postponed because some dependency was not known until a few days before the retirement date?

The data migration plan is a living document subject to additional information during the project's progression. You cannot expect the entire plan to be ready with all ten components as a prerequisite for commencing data migration activities, such as data discovery and developing data transformation logic/code for data migration. However, before you write a single piece of code or buy expensive software licenses for data migration, a first approved version (Data Migration Plan 1.0) should be ready with the choices available and decisions made about the first three foundational components of the framework.

The first version of the plan should include a high-level summary of decisions and choices for the remaining seven components. Data Migration Plan 1.0 is a strategic document for the stakeholders to review and endorse. Add or amend the remaining seven components in the plan with business rules and decisions made with the project progression. Multiple templates for the data migration plan are one Google search away. However, I found them overwhelming as a one-off document covering all facets of the data migration before the project initiation. I can recall my struggles in the early days (as data migration lead) in drafting a data migration plan using ready-made templates that were not directly applicable to my project.

During legacy decommissioning projects, the data migration workstream deals with an unknown source (legacy system with limited support and documentation) and a moving target (ongoing customizations of the target system). Therefore, waiting for correct business rules for mapping or finalizing a robust downstream integration design for the data migration plan could cause significant delays. On the other hand, data migration test runs could introduce new mapping or data quality gaps after the stakeholders endorsed the data migration plan. Such gaps would require forming business rules and risk mitigation analysis with controls implemented for data migration, subject to documentation (record management) in a regulatory-sensitive environment.

The first version of the plan sets the foundation for the initial test run or data migration iteration. As the project progresses, decisions are made in the remaining components, each decision a valuable contribution towards decommissioning, which should be documented and agreed upon. The plan's final version, which all stakeholders should endorse before decommissioning the legacy system, serves as the organizational knowledge base. It provides retrospective information about how business data were migrated from the legacy system, underscoring the strategic value of the Data Migration Plan as more than just a courtesy document.

With the data migration framework introduced as a strategic instrument and the significance of the data migration plan explored to bring the framework to life, let's examine the framework components in the following chapters.

CHAPTER 2

Data Migration Scope

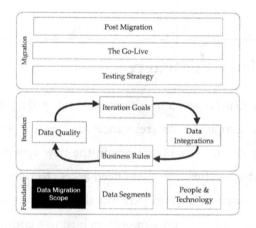

Defining the scope of data to be migrated into the new system is the most significant activity when decommissioning legacy business systems with decades(s) of transactional data. This activity is not merely a technical task; it involves a comprehensive assessment of the sheer volume of legacy data. It addresses business questions about what data should be migrated, what data should be retained, and what legacy data can be purged or archived. It is a cross-functional business decision where stakeholders from multiple business units, especially operational experts, data management leadership, and the legal or compliance lead, should be involved. Let's dig deeper.

Prevent decision paralysis and avoid the lazy approach of "Let's migrate everything," which has a high potential to become a risk magnet of inefficiencies bundled with cost and delays in the new system deployed after investing millions. Rather, think logically and assess the amount of legacy data needed in the new system based on Operational Continuity and Compliance Adherence.

Operational Continuity

The most critical section criteria for legacy data to be in the migration scope is its relevance to ensure uninterrupted continuity of business operations in the new system post legacy retirement when business users need access to relevant open and closed transaction data to perform their jobs effectively. Some mundane examples of post-migration business continuity are:

- Patients are admitted via the legacy hospital system but are to be discharged from the new system.

- Scheduling an appointment in the new system for a patient from the waiting list created by the legacy patient management system.

- A clinician wants to access the last appointment notes of a patient with an annual follow-up appointment. But the last notes were captured in the legacy patient management system.

- An order is captured in the legacy system, but items sold are dispatched from the new system.

- Users want to access a customer's sales history, including the last time the customer purchased an item three years ago when the legacy system was operational.

- A home loan application is captured in the legacy system at a bank, but the assessment process commences in the new banking system.

You must assess and consider the data you need immediately, within hours, days, weeks, months, and at least a year after retiring the legacy system. Legacy data of open and recent transactions are a must-have in the migration scope to avoid interruptions in processing ongoing business operations on the cutover day. You must also anticipate future events that may need data captured during the days when the legacy system was operational:

- **Factor in the number of instances of the legacy system.** When evaluating the impact of data migration scope selection on business continuity, it is essential to consider the number of instances of the legacy system. You need to clarify whether there is a single centralized instance or multiple instances of legacy systems at various business locations with different lifespans and any past or present integrations, including manual data reconciliation between business sites. If there are several instances of the legacy system, you will encounter challenges reconciling duplicate records and ensuring data consistency in the new system [4]. For example, if a customer or patient record exists in multiple legacy system instances, you need to establish business rules that specify which record is deemed the most current. We have a whole chapter dedicated to business rules. Don't panic now!

- **Factor in migration approach, whether Big Bang or Phased.** Secondly, it is essential to consider the decommissioning approach while assessing the migration scope, whether it will be phased or big bang. This decision is not only based on the volume of legacy data; it also considers the complexity of change management, which includes timely communication and training for a significant number of people affected by the system change. Change Management itself is a separate subject on its own, with profound research and best-practices literature available on it. I have also shed some light on change management in Chapter 12, "The Larger Picture." For now, note that there is no rule of thumb, such as a big bang for a centralized legacy system and phased for multiple instances or vice versa.

The order and nature of the decommissioning process (phased or big bang) should be evaluated carefully based on the business needs and appetite to handle enterprise-wide system change. The number of legacy instances, data migration scope defined, and chosen decommissioning approach directly correlate with business continuity, which depends on downstream data integrations from the legacy system to other operational systems, data aggregation platforms, and reporting solutions. Therefore, cautiously assess the feasibility, viability, and desirability of keeping two systems running with the Phased approach or jumping into a new world in one big push with the Big Bang (and Drum Rolls!).

Compliance Adherence

Legacy data on historical or closed business transactions and demographics of the entities related to that past transaction qualify to be in the migration scope to ensure adherence to laws and regulations (generic and industry-specific) or industry guidelines and policies about legacy data retention.

While you define what is in the scope for migration, you must address decisions about legacy data archival or purging methods. From a business analyst's perspective, you can live happily with only three years of historical data in the new system. However, your legal team may suggest migrating the last seven years of data to comply with a particular data retention law (at the national or state level) or industry-specific policy [5].

In the context of health data retention, the most common practice is to retain records for a minimum of ten years in the new health record and patient management system. This period is measured from the day after the most recent date indicated in the patient's health information, which reflects the date on which health services were last provided to the patient. Within New Zealand, where I had the first-hand experience of ferreting out the data migration scope, I was enlightened about the comprehensive rights of patients and the obligations of medical practitioners regarding medical records outlined in several pieces of legislation, including the Privacy Act 1993(and 2020), the Health Act 1956, and the Health Information Privacy Code 1994.

Evaluate Your Options

With the two criteria for data migration scope explained above, let me expand on the ten-year example of healthcare data. In this case, for uninterrupted business continuity and to prevent delays in health service delivery to patients due to glitches in the patient management system, you must migrate all the data about the patient and health services provided to those who are actively under the care (outpatient and inpatient) without any discharge date or referral closed date attached to their current episode of care and future appointments scheduled. However, adhering to the data retention policy, you would also need legacy data from the last ten years when the patient was discharged or services provided within the prior ten years from the cutover date.

The last ten years are a calendar year or financial year. Which particular date attribute you should use to denote the most recent date in the patient's health information is also subject to discussion, debate, and decision. It could be the discharge date for inpatients, the referral closed date for outpatients, or the medical coding date captured after any health service is provided in the last updated timestamp on the patient's medical record. Another key point is that the scope is calculated from the day of cutover. For example, the scope of the last ten years means data accumulated from 1st July 2012 for the planned cutover date of 1st July 2022. Factor this in when planning an incremental or phased decommissioning with multiple cutover dates for the legacy system — gradual decommissioning by business unit/department/site over a period of time with different date ranges in the migration scope for each cutover.

In the last chapter, "The Larger Picture," I have covered how having formal data governance practices can be of great value to removing tech-debt with minimized risk. However, it is worth noting that organizations with higher data governance maturity and lifecycle management would have an enterprise data architect or a similar role. Such a stakeholder could rightly recommend leveraging existing data archival policies for archival and purging the out-of-scope data, liaising with data and information teams on refactoring existing integrations and assisting the data migration team in identifying critical data for migration scope. In diverse cases, which are also likely to be the most common, the stakeholders may expect data archival decisions and reporting refactoring to be a part of the deliverables from the decommissioning project. Therefore, I recommend verifying these stakeholder expectations early on and documenting risk assessment of the scope selected, articulating each risk with its impact and likelihood on the business.

After accommodating all the needs and suggestions of various stakeholders, you will have multiple options for scope selection, each with a distinct set of risks and benefits. Leverage the data migration plan to propose all possibilities and capture the stakeholder's decision on the option picked.

Quantitative and qualitative risk analysis are well-established fields with extensive literature available. If you are unfamiliar with risk management as a discipline, I recommend starting with the Project Management Institute's article on this topic [6]. It is worth exploring whether existing risk management practices can be leveraged to manage risks arising from decisions made during data migration activities. Large, regulated enterprises often have a formal enterprise risk management framework based on the OWASP Risk Rating Methodology [7], while IT security teams may already have standalone risk management practices for their projects.

Assessing the risks associated with data migration scope helps estimate the severity of potential risks stemming from different scope choices. The severity of any risk is typically defined by two factors: **impact**—the adverse effect a risk could have on the project or business—and **likelihood**—the probability of the risk materializing. Likelihood is often measured on a five-level scale, such as **1 = very unlikely, 2 = low likelihood, 3 = likely, 4 = highly likely, and 5 = near certain**. The **impact** of a risk (sometimes referred to as its consequence) is also defined using a discrete scale, such as **1 = very low, 2 = low, 3 = medium, 4 = high, and 5 = very high**.

There is no strict requirement to use a five-level scale; other scales may be applied. However, many professionals find that five levels provide a practical balance—offering more granularity than a basic three-level scale (low/medium/high) without the complexity of a more detailed 10-level scale.

The initial version of the data migration plan should outline all potential options for the migration scope, along with the option proposed or selected by stakeholders. This includes defining the proportion of legacy data within the migration scope and determining the decommissioning approach— whether **Big Bang** or **Phased**. Below is an example of how to articulate different options for defining the data migration scope, incorporating qualitative risk analysis and potential mitigations. This is intended purely as an example and should not be considered a one-size-fits-all solution. However, it can serve as a starting point for conducting a risk assessment of the data migration scope in your project.

Option 1: Big Bang—Full Data Migration

Sounds Like: *Let's migrate everything in one go across all sites.*

Risks:
1. High volume of irrelevant or redundant data inflates costs and time.
2. Data quality issues in legacy data carry over to the new system.
3. Overwhelming system performance.
4. Long duration for the data migration on the cutover date resulting in longer down time.

Likelihood: High

Impact: High

Mitigation: Select a different option. Not a viable choice.

Option 2: Big Bang—Partial Data Migration, Only Open Transactions

Sounds Like: *Let's migrate only open transactions across all sites in one go.*

Risks:
1. Missed critical data of closed transactions needed for business continuity.
2. Stakeholder disagreements on what constitutes open transaction.

3. Future costs for retrieving or deleting un-migrated data from the legacy or archival system.

4. Violation of data retention and data privacy policies.

Likelihood: High

Impact: High

Mitigation: Select a different option.

Option 3: Big Bang—All Open and Time-bound Closed Transactions (last ten years)

Sounds Like: *Let's migrate everything entered the legacy system in the last ten years from the decommissioning date, across all sites in one go.*

Risks:

1. Long duration for data migration on the cutover date, resulting in longer down time.

2. Stakeholder disagreements on what constitutes an open transaction.

3. Refactoring of data reporting and analytics solutions.

Likelihood: Medium

Impact: Low

Mitigation:

1. Split the data migration activity on the cutover date between open and closed transactions to reduce downtime. Migrate only open transactions on the cutover day, followed by closed transactions after the new system is live.

2. Organize workshops and clarify the definition of what constitutes an open transaction.

3. Assess refactoring efforts for reporting and analytical needs and allocate funds for it within the decommissioning budget.

Option 4: Phased—All Open and Time-bound Closed Transactions (last ten years)

Sounds Like: *Let's migrate everything entered the legacy system in the last ten years from the decommissioning date, few sites at a time as phased rollout over a period.*

Risks:

1. Multiple data migrations and cutovers over a period with both target and legacy systems operational simultaneously cause double entries and manual reconciliations.

2. Stakeholder disagreements on what constitutes an open transaction.

3. Refactoring of data reporting and analytics solutions.

Likelihood: Medium

Impact: Low

Mitigation:

1. Define each migration phase clearly by business location or business units with minimum overlapping between data needs.

2. Organize workshops and clarify the definition of what constitutes an open transaction.

3. Assess refactoring efforts for reporting and analytical needs and allocate funds within the decommissioning budget.

Decisions made here in the first foundational component will feed subsequent components of the framework.

By implementing the first foundational component of the data migration framework with diligence and foresight, organizations can pave the way for a smooth transition to the new system that enhances operational efficiency, ensures compliance, and positions them for future growth rather than creating disappointments, delays and frustrations and encouraging employees to wonder about the purpose of life.

Questions to Ask

Each chapter ends with a series of questions for stakeholders to address, and the data migration plan should reflect the answers within the component of the data migration framework described in that chapter.

The first component of the plan, namely the data migration scope, should answer the following questions:

- Can we quantify the volume of data to be migrated to the new system, and what is the reasoning behind this volume?

- Is there a single legacy system or multiple instances at different locations?

- Should we migrate all data across the enterprise in one go or take a cautious, phased approach with multiple small migrations?

- What are the pros and cons of the big-bang and phased approach?

- If multiple instances of the legacy system are running, what would be the most logical order for decommissioning them?

- What would happen to the data outside the scope, and what if we need the out-of-scope historical data in the future while it is not available in the new business system?

- What information about the legacy system's data structures is available via system documentation or data dictionaries?

- What is the status of in-house or vendor-based technical support for data archival and purging?

CHAPTER 3

Data Segments

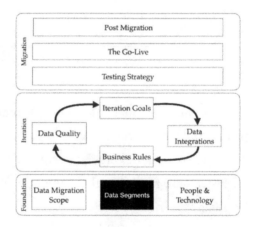

While the framework's scope component ferrets out the correct quantity of legacy data necessary for migration, the following foundation component focuses on a qualitative analysis of the legacy data within the migration scope to segregate the data into logical partitions and orchestrate the order of data migration with the due diligence activities to comply with regulations and policies while migrating the data.

Critical business applications such as ERPs and CRMs from different vendors within the same domain (e.g., healthcare, FMCG, logistics, etc.) can vary in functionalities and features. However, the underlying data in any business application from any vendor can be seen in two logical segments, namely Master Data and Transactional Data. You cannot capture transactional data in a business application until master data is available. Data transformation code generated for the legacy data migration is nothing but the expression of how data structures of these two types of data are mapped between the legacy source system and the new target system.

Master Data

Master data, for instance, includes data about customers, patients, products, stores, employees, service or device locations, and many more that represent core entities crucial to conducting a business transaction. Master data facilitates the foundational details that form the basis of any business operation. Such data stays relatively stable with a lower frequency of change. For example, you don't update a customer or a patient's address or phone number every week in your system, and you don't change product prices daily. To capture data about a sale in the business system, you need the customer and product already in the system. Therefore, customer and product data are the master data.

Along with the core business entities, master data also includes referential data, such as lookup values for gender codes or product categories, locations, wards and beds, a list of health services provided at a hospital, and a list of business units or departments. This data also tends to change less frequently and is essential for configuring a business system. For example, in a hospital setup, you need to load all wards and the location of beds in a new hospital management system before the system can be operationalized. I see such referential and configurational data as master data in data migration. Unlike patients and customers, referential or configurational data are not always subject to migration; they can be manually loaded into the target system as a part of the configuration task. However, the correct and approved mapping from old to new codes is a key ingredient for the data migration code.

Transactional Data

Transactional data represents a business transaction, such as a sales order, quote, medical appointment, or waiting list entry. When defining the scope of data migration, we are actually addressing the amount of past and current business transactions worth migrating to the new system for smooth operations. Data about core business entities implicitly becomes part of the data migration scope if they are involved in those past and current transactions chosen for migration. In my first project, the scope of migration was all patients and activities associated with referrals received within the last seven financial years from the cutover date. I derived a distinct list of patient identifiers from referral data in the legacy system to extract precise patient data from the legacy system necessary for migration.

Transactional data typically involves intricate relationships with master data and other transactional data. For example, a single sales order can be associated with multiple products, a specific customer, a designated salesperson, or an outpatient visit is a quarterly follow-up visit after a surgery that was scheduled from a waiting list. These intricate relationships in business transactions captured in the past must be accurately identified and maintained during the migration process to ensure that the integrity of these relationships remains intact and functional in the new system.

Migrate the Master Data First

Data migration between applications is executed as multiple test runs (iterations) before the decommissioning date. I will cover how to plan test iterations in Chapter 8. However, I would like to highlight that your data migration plan should propose migrating master data first during the initial test runs. For example, migrate the product catalog and customers first, followed by historical and open sales orders, or migrate patients and wards before past and current inpatient visits. The approach to migrate master data first should also touch upon the necessary referential or configurational data to be mapped between the legacy system and the target business application.

The target system's data structure dictates the data transformation efforts for successful data migration. The target system can have logical data constructs unavailable in the legacy system. Dealing with master data first can highlight logical gaps between old and new data structures that demand business rules-driven data transformation. In my example of the last seven years of referrals, the legacy patient management system from 1993 had no concept of referrals for inpatients, which turned into a showstopper because the entire process flow in the target system starts with a referral. Unlike outpatient visits, it immediately prevented me from migrating patients from past and current inpatient visits due to the lack of parent referrals in the legacy system.

After the legacy system is decommissioned, each inpatient visit recorded in the new system will always be associated with a referral. The limitation of the legacy system caused the risk of missing patients from the migration scope who have had only inpatient visits, which could have catastrophic impacts. Raised early on with the vendor and stakeholders, a business rule was timely constructed to produce dummy referrals on the fly for each inpatient visit in the migration scope with clear flags that make it easy for downstream integrations to ignore dummy referrals from their respective processes. Implementing these dummy referrals was technically easy, but bringing all stakeholders on one page to form a business rule can be challenging for the project manager.

Focusing on master data first will expose such showstoppers early on in the project, giving enough time for decision-makers to analyze and react appropriately with either a business rule for data migration or a change request for a vendor. Note that I am not suggesting that migrating master data first is easy compared to transactional data. However, issues and gaps addressed during master data migration will speed up the migration of transactional legacy data in hindsight, with most of the groundwork and decisions done for data migration.

Migrating master data first can also feed back into migrating transaction data. For example, in my project, I had to first migrate health providers' and teams' data for the target system to generate unique identifiers of individual doctors and their teams, which are then mapped with the legacy codes of doctors and teams. The mapping of legacy and new codes is a prerequisite for transforming legacy transactional data such as past inpatient visits that capture which team of doctors was primarily responsible for an inpatient during a critical surgery.

Please consider that you are highly likely to deal with a moving target with customizations and new developments under progress in the selected target system. Customizations in the target system are highly expected to alter the data structures of the target system and may introduce or drop new columns/attributes in the migration process. You can't postpone data migration until all customizations are done in the target system. Therefore, it's necessary to get precise prerequisites from the vendor for commencing data migration with the master data and having an up-to-date data migration test environment where migrated data can be tested swiftly through the user interface of the target application. Note that having a testing environment for data migration can incur some infrastructure costs. Can you be smart and conduct User Acceptance Testing (UAT) with real migrated data? Maybe yes. But please consult with your legal or compliance teams.

In my first data migration project, target data structures of transactional data such as appointments, past visits, and waiting lists were changing every fortnight with the latest release of the target system for User Acceptance Testing (UAT). Comparatively, the target data structures of patients, health providers, employees, and teams were stable. Lesser changes to the User Interface (UI) for CRUD (Create, Read, Update, and Delete) operations on master data allowed us (the project team) to test the data migration process with master data at the very initial stage of data migration code development. I could not produce all the mandatory patient data in my first few test runs. I leveraged a lot of UNKNOWNS, Nulls, and default values as temporary placeholders where mapping was complex or demanded more discovery and analysis. How I kept track of temporary placeholders and replaced them with business rules is covered in Chapters 5 and 8. However, the key point I want to convey here is I had enough low-hanging fruits in the patient's master data to build a simple data migration development (Extract, Transform, and Load or ETL for short) environment, test the process, build trust in the process, and get going with a scalable solution.

Within my first few months on the first project, I was able to report on the success ratio of migrating patients to the new system with reasons for failures. My concise reporting style was, "If the cutover were today, we would have successfully migrated only 26 patients out of 100 in the scope due to X, Y, and Z predominant issues and a few additional issues subject to further analysis." It got the ball moving, and a process was established to raise showstoppers, decision limbos, and time-consuming data transformation tasks that hindered the data migration progress.

Concluding master data migration early in the initial test runs can facilitate data migration testing for master data at an early stage of the project. A quicker feedback loop of data migration from the beginning can instill trust in your decommissioning efforts while uncovering major pitfalls early on. The practice of data migration testing from the early stage of the project can avoid situations where you only have weeks, days, or hours left with the last penny in the budget to conduct the "robust and thorough" data migration testing before the cutover.

Looking at the legacy data in master and transactional also opens opportunities to deviate from the legacy system as a source of truth for the master data. Timeworn and deteriorated operational legacy systems are not ideally used for reporting due to performance issues. However, they feed much transactional data for reporting and analytics as periodic CSV extracts. An existing data warehouse (data mart or lakehouse) could be a better source of master data if good quality controls are built on the data extracted from the legacy system daily or weekly. Do not reinvent the wheel. Focus on creating a good engine instead if you already have the wheel. If extracting master data from the existing data warehouse is more reliable and manageable than the legacy system itself, refresh the data warehouse one last time from the source system before running the data migration on the cutover day—more on cutover nuances in Chapter 10.

Another alternative for the master data in the scope of the migration could be integrated systems where partial operations of the legacy systems are already offloaded to more recent business applications with contemporary tech stacks. There is no harm in assessing such parallel business applications as potential data sources for the master data within the scope of migration. You will need collaboration from your data and system experts. Applying the DMBOK framework for integration and interpretability for this problem also recommends onboarding current data architects, data modelers, data stewards, ETL, and service and interface developers [8].

With the information provided above, I hope you will be prepared with precise questions on the agenda when you invite them to the project discovery meeting as a project or program manager. We will look into the people part in the next chapter in detail.

With the context provided above, the data migration plan based on the framework should articulate the logical partition of the legacy data and propose the data migration order to the stakeholders.

The consensus on migrating master first, followed by transactional, will steer the planning, prioritization, and execution of business rules, test iterations, and testing strategy, along with identifying key measures to monitor data migration progress.

Data migration for retiring legacy systems is an old problem, and multiple research papers advocate migrating master data first. I highly recommend the paper "Patterns for data migration projects" by Martin Wagner and Tim Wellhausen, first published in 2010 at the 15th European Conference on Pattern Languages of Programs, which articulates the same logic while recommending to migrate the legacy data along domain partitions [10]. The introduction of cloud and SaaS has added a new dimension to the data migration problem. However, the fundamental challenges of data migration are the same as reflected in several research papers from the early 2000s[11] and 2010s [12]. I have cited all research papers in the bibliography that support my recommendation.

Compliance Adherence

In the first foundational component of the framework, policies and compliances related to legacy data retention are factored in to define the scope of data migration. Leverage the second foundational component of the framework for one more due diligence with the legal, compliance, and information security teams. Once you identify the data segments and the nature of the data in migration, verify all applicable regulatory and policy compliances on the storage, movement, and processing of legacy data. Data and information-related regulations across the globe usually cover the following data categories [13]:

- Personal Identification Information (PII)
- Financially Sensitive Data
- Medically Sensitive Data/Personal Health Information
- Educational Records.

If legacy data under the migration scope includes one or more categories listed above, I recommend acquiring legal advice before commencing any data transformation activities. Some vendors provide data migration services where they take a backup of the entire legacy database and do all the magic at their end. It's a great and less painful data migration, but please check with your legal or compliance team before dumping data on the vendor's doormat.

In such a "Give me everything, I'll do the rest" migration approach by the vendor, the legal team can suggest necessary contractual obligations with the vendor that ensure the destruction of the legacy database post-data migration. Dig deeper, find, and disclose all regulations and policies data migration processes must comply with, such as regulations related to the use of personal information, disclosure of personal information, disclosure outside national and state legislative boundaries, and unique identifiers.

During a data migration project, business data could move out of the organization and be subject to auditable adherence to confidentiality and regulatory compliance. Even if you are hosting the application in-house within the private network for production, during the data migration test runs, data may move to a sandbox environment hosted by the vendor. Thus, we investigate and address data regulations and policies in the foundational work before commencing data migration activities.

Controls implemented to meet compliance could introduce data encryption or obfuscation in the ETL process before the data is transmitted from the organization's network boundaries. Secondly, policy-based restrictions on PII access may limit the number of users available for screen-to-screen data migration testing who are authorized to access the personal data of your patients, customers, employees, or suppliers.

If you are already in an environment with regulatory sensitive data and mature data governance practices, leverage existing data classifications and relative data management policies to be applied to the legacy data during the migration process. While elaborating on the second component of the framework in the data migration plan, you can add a concise tabular view of the data segment and all relevant data regulations applied to it, as well as a reference to policies followed and controls implemented. An example is in Table 1 below.

It should be obvious that the first version of the data migration plan discusses the foundational discovery and groundwork needed to execute data migration. Addressing data regulations and policies within the first two components of the data migration plan will allow you to perform necessary due diligence with your legal and compliance stakeholders during the discovery phase of the decommissioning project.

Data Segment	Regulation	Policies	Controls in ETL/Vendor Contract
Master Patient Data	Privacy Act NZ 2020	HDT_POL_003	Contractual Obligation
	Health (Retention of Health Information) Regulations 1996	-	Patient with death date within the last seven years from cutover are within the migration scope.
...	...	...	...
...	...	...	...

Table 1: Data Segments and Relative Controls to Meet Compliance

> *The reactive involvement of legal and compliance teams after the migration that has already caused regulatory violations is not a great situation to be in as a project lead or sponsor.*

Questions to Ask

The second component of the plan, namely the data segments, should answer the following questions:

- Can we identify and differentiate business data in the migration scope into logical segments, such as master and transaction data?

- When can we start data migration activities during the decommissioning project's life cycle?

- What legacy data are low-hanging fruits that can be migrated in the first test run?

- Do we have alternative data sources, such as a data warehouse or another business system, for the master data within the scope of migration?

- Is complete data migration offered as a managed service by the vendor of the target system?

- Shall we wait for the data migration testing until all data is entirely migrated to the new application, or shall we start the data migration testing in phases early on?

- What types of regulatory and policy compliances are applied to the legacy data within the migration scope?

- How do we ensure the data migration test runs do not violate data compliance?

- Can we ethically use real data without privacy violations for the data migration testing with screen-to-screen comparisons?

CHAPTER 4

People and Technology

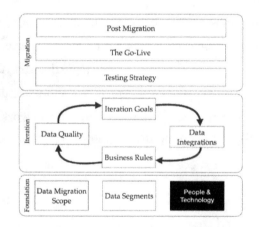

We are now on the last foundational component of the Data Migration Framework that you should address during the project discovery stage before a single piece of code is written for data migration. All three foundational components are intertwined where the first two components of the framework focus on the scope, segments, and regulations of the legacy data, and the third component of the framework liaises with stakeholders in identifying and mitigating risks stemming from resource availability and selection of technology for data migration.

Figure 2: Data Migration Framework - Foundation

The above three foundational components are not mutually exclusive nor sequential as such. You need the right people mentioned in this chapter to find answers to the first two components. The combined set of questions from all three foundational components of the framework can set the scope of the discovery work to be conducted and summarized for stakeholders as the first deliverable of the decommissioning project. I propose this first deliverable to be the first version of the data migration plan, which stakeholders should endorse. If you are at the planning stage, leverage this framework and equip yourself with actionable information to allocate the proper funds and resources for successful decommissioning.

Under the People and Technology component of the framework, this chapter articulates challenges with people and possibilities with technology when migrating data from a legacy system. We will assess the availability of technical and business experts, look at tools available to execute data migration, and estimate the ability and capacity of your experts to work with a selected tool or work along with data engineers/developers tasked with data migration development.

We, the People

Stakeholders will make or break your migration.

Data migration is not just an IT project—it's a political battlefield. Business users care about operational continuity, compliance teams care about regulations, and executives care about cost. If you don't align stakeholders early, you'll face:

- Conflicting priorities that delay decisions.
- Last-minute objections that derail timelines.
- Finger-pointing when things go wrong.

The solution? Data Migration is a business problem. Solve it like a one!

Involve key stakeholders from Day 1. Treat data migration as an organization-wide initiative, not just an IT task.

Over several years of professional life, I observed and learned a few things about people leadership while being a part of effective, average, and below-average teams. I am not the first to realize that people, processes, and technology are the three foundations of any project, product, or service delivery. However, I feel that the process and technology components have evolved over centuries since we entered the industrial age, which is now entering the fourth industrial revolution ("Industry 4.0") era. Meanwhile, the People part has been consistent forever and influenced the execution of processes and technology. That could be why people management lessons in *How to Win and Influence People* by Dale Carnegie 1936 are still relevant in this bestselling self-help book.

In hindsight, I realized that decommissioning a legacy system is more of a people problem than a technology problem. When a business system runs over decades and manages core business transactions, various business units/departments in an enterprise could depend highly on the legacy system with a few in-house system matter experts (SMEs). In my experience, I also came across people who have only worked on the legacy system in their entire career spanning over twenty to twenty-five years. Data migration is a subset of a more considerable enterprise-wide change that touches many people in an organization.

> *You are adorable if you believe everyone affected by the change will react similarly with great enthusiasm.*

Not everyone is happy about the change. Some may want to drag the legacy system forever to justify their role in your organization. Therefore, do not assume or take for granted the availability and desirability of in-house SMEs to support decommissioning efforts actively. You may be lucky to have incredible human beings as your business and technology SMEs. Still, they could be super occupied and busy with their Business-As-Usual (BAU) and operational duties with limited or no spare time to support the decommissioning project team.

Collaboration and input from the business SMEs are essential for forming business rules, mapping rules, and data cleansing approaches to execute robust data migration and ensure smooth business continuity post-migration. They have answers for how a business system is used and historical amendments done, what workarounds and ad-hoc processes have been implemented over the years in the legacy system, what downstream dependencies pose a significant risk for business continuity, any possibility of regulatory violations due to data migration activities, and many more nuances about the business impact of the legacy system.

Even for the managed data migration services by the vendor, one would need support from in-house business and technical SMEs such as super-senior business or system analysts, legacy application admins, DBAs, architects, IT leadership, and data governance teams (if any) to migrate legacy data accurately and securely. According to the DMBOK framework, you would need varying degrees of participation from various people with the following roles or duties in your organization. You may not have everyone listed here for best-case scenarios. Please list all the potential people in your organization with these roles or similar responsibilities and assess their availability for the data migration project:

- Data producers (team leaders of people behind data entry)

- IT steering committee
- Subject Matter Experts (SMEs)
- Data architects
- Business and data analyst
- Data modelers
- Database admin and developer
- ETL, service, interface developers
- Yourself (executives and managers).

Awesome Technology

If the target system is known for the decommissioning project or a few candidates are under evaluation, assess the level of support and resources available for data migration activities from the vendor of the new system. In some cases, the vendor can provide complete data migration as a managed service, given that the raw source data is made available to them, which is subject to compliance risk, as covered in the previous chapter. In other instances, the vendor would provide a means or a way to load data into the target system, which mainly includes three options:

- Populate CSV or Excel files with cleaned and transformed legacy data to be migrated. The target system ingests data from files.

- Populate a SQL database with pre-defined tables from which the target system can ingest data.

- Push data straight into the target system using RESTful APIs.

Based on the available load method in the target system, choose potential ETL tools and technology to execute data extraction and transformation of source data from the legacy system into the data structure required by the load method of the given target system. Whether you build a data migration development environment on-premises or rent out infrastructure in any cloud offerings, tools and technology will incur a cost. One can also choose to onboard specialized data migration software and consultants for managed services such as Hopp or BridgeHead to minimize the risk stemming from decommissioning. The vendor of the target system could also recommend specialized software for data migration that works best with their application.

I want to mention Hopp explicitly here when covering data migration technology. I was fortunate to work on data migration software Hopp first-hand during their early years in the business around 2017-18. They have grown by leaps and bounds over the last ten years since their inception, and I can confidently recommend their solution. I resonate with them because their data migration solution is designed to solve a business problem, not just a data problem.

Founders of Hopp reached out to me after I wrote my first article on data migration in 2017, and I shared it with different data management groups on LinkedIn. Although I used SQL Server Integration Services (SSIS) as the ETL tool and wrote PL/SQL and

T-SQL code for data extraction and transformation, applying my lessons learned on the Hopp platform further expanded my perspective on seeing data migration as a business problem and leveraging specialized data migration tools like Hopp instead of relying on generic ETL solutions such as SSIS, DBT or Informatica. I cannot express enough gratitude to Sune Visti Petersen, Managing Director and the Founder of Hopp, who has played a significant role in my professional growth and spared his valuable time for interviews with me for this book.

You can't miss the marketplace when it comes to data migration tools. Over the last decade, with the rise of cloud-native business applications, a marketplace has emerged for major ERPs and CRMs such as Salesforce, Oracle Fusion, SAP, or Temenos, where you can buy add-on apps that work in tandem with significant business applications. For example, Hopp is already in the marketplace of Temenos – a leading digital banking solution [14].

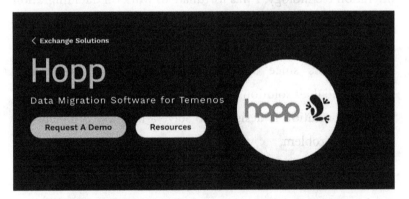

Figure 3: Marketplace Example - Hopp on Temenos Exchange

I elaborated on Hopp because I worked on the tool and saw their journey. However, I do not want this book to be a sales pitch for a solution. Therefore, I am spotlighting a few more tools I found to be widely used data migration solutions in my research. These tools are designed to facilitate seamless data migration, ensuring data integrity and operational continuity during transitions between systems:

- **Midas.** Bodhtree's cloud-centric data migration solution streamlines the integration process with Salesforce, SAP, MySQL, Oracle databases, and various ERP systems. It is designed for two-way integration between intricate workflows and customer journeys. https://tinyurl.com/psm7dhdf

- **InCountry**. A comprehensive solution for migrating data across borders into Salesforce Hyperforce. It supports complex Salesforce schemas and large file attachments and ensures data integrity during migration. https://tinyurl.com/mvfjp7hx

- **ChainSys**. Provides data quality, profiling, and built-in reconciliation with over 3,000 migration adapters ready for SAP, Oracle, Salesforce, and Procore. It's designed to handle large-scale migrations with high accuracy. https://tinyurl.com/y9bxwc7e

- **Rapid4Cloud.** Offers automated tools for migrating data to Oracle SaaS applications, providing out-of-the-box support for Oracle E-Business Suite as a source application. https://tinyurl.com/4b2a7hkf

- **Meddbase Data Migration Toolkit.** This tool facilitates the direct import of data into the Medbase application. It supports bulk uploads of patient demographics, scanned documents, medical images, and comprehensive medical records while ensuring accurate mapping and integration into the new system. https://tinyurl.com/mrh6b7xv

- **MediQuant's Data Migration Solution.** MediQuant offers tools to extract, structure, and map complete patient and employee data from retired systems, facilitating seamless transitions to new platforms while maintaining data integrity. https://tinyurl.com/2ruswbtb

With the marketplace, major vendors have already built a community of service and solution providers around them. Therefore, look for what is already available and recommended by the vendor if you deploy a multi-million-dollar system from a well-known vendor. This chapter aims to showcase all technology options and avoid any silver bullet choice. Evaluate available tools per your needs to find the best solution. Going with traditional ETL tools or manual data entry in the new system could be good choices in some circumstances where legacy data is not complex or tiny in size.

You wouldn't use a chainsaw to trim delicate rose bushes in your garden—it's overkill for the task and could cause more harm than good. But when dealing with a large forest of trees to be cut down, a chainsaw becomes indispensable. Similarly, an ETL tool might suffice for simple data migration tasks. However, when the complexity increases and the scale of effort becomes significant, relying on a specialized data migration tool like Hopp can make all the difference.

The Right Mix of People and Technology

The older the legacy system, the darker the fun of decommissioning it. Data migration is a special event and not business as usual—they are short-lived and one-off, but inevitable. Apart from the deterioration of the system, mergers and acquisitions can also force legacy system decommissioning. This unique, one-off, yet critical task needs a special task force behind it with the right tools. Although you know what type of people you need and what kind of technologies are available in the market, resource planning for data migration will depend on the organization's culture and data management maturity.

If you are an outsider at the helm of a decommissioning project or an evidence-based decision-maker, it would not harm you to undertake a Data Management Maturity Assessment (DMMA) of current data management practices at your organization. The outcome of the maturity assessment should identify critical gaps that can assist in making sound choices for the right balance between business and technical resources required for successful data migration. With five as the lowest and one being the highest, with a higher maturity level (2 and above) backed by well-established data management practices and well-documented business context, you can rely on ETL tools and technical folks to lead data migration with business SMEs participating as internal consultants with limited capacity. I tagged this path as **the technology-led approach**.

With a lower maturity level (3 and below) and limited technical resources, I recommend bringing in specialized data migration software and external consultants to assist the business SMEs leading the decommissioning challenge—**the business-led approach** to data migration. Training business SMEs on a data migration tool could eat up some time and funds, but it is a good investment for the long term as it will set a consistency for the language and tool across all stakeholders involved in data migration.

Data migration projects with lower DMMA outcomes demand more time for discovery work in the source system to track and handle changes and ad hoc workarounds implemented over decades of operational use. While writing this, I recall a few amusing and entertaining détournements people invented to utilize a data field on the UI for something completely different— truly avant-garde!

The unknown nature of source databases, poor data quality, and orphan business processes are common symptoms of lower data management maturity, which requires significant efforts for discovery and reconciliation for data migration. In such a case, having your business SMEs take charge of data migration with external technical consultants with proven tools could be more fruitful than relying on two introverted database developers working in a silo on some ETL tool.

Various proven DMMA frameworks are available to determine your organization's maturity level. The scope of DMMA ranges from a single process to overall enterprise-wide data management. DMMA can be further narrowed down within data management to particular areas such as data security, business intelligence, data architecture, or data integration. DMMA is a broader topic worth a dedicated book on its own. DMBOK includes a dedicated chapter on DMMA, a concise and comprehensive resource on this topic [15]. I also want to recommend "Comparison of Data Management Maturity Assessments (DMMA)" prepared by the dedicated folks at the Data Strategy Professionals [16].

If you are an insider and old rice in the organization, close your eyes, put your hands on your heart and ask yourself what maturity tag you would give to your data management culture from the following options:

1. Champion
2. Achiever
3. Player

4. Mediocre

5. Looser.

The hidden advantage of the above maturity levels is that those who realize their rigid culture is highly likely to be at level 4 or 5 would first raise questions on the appropriate word selection and may prefer "Laggards," "Lagger," or something softer. If you advocate for softer words for level 4 or 5, I am assured your organization is definitely at level 4 or below without any assessment. I have just saved your money on maturity assessment right here. I would call it the ROI of my book. Put the saved funds from DMMA into a business-led approach and accordingly onboard the right tools and key people for the successful data migration.

In data migration for business applications, we do not simply migrate data, but transform it from a legacy structure to a new structure, which includes dependencies and relationships that can introduce a lot of complexity and frustration with a lower data management maturity level. After my first successful data migration, the next project I worked on as a consultant was because their ETL developer was gone after creating a spaghetti of code and data flows over a year that was difficult to decipher.

In my interview with Sune from Hopp, he also elaborated on a project from South Africa where his client had lost their primary ETL developer after two years, who left a massive pile of SQL and ETL code with no documentation. In that case, two years' worth of development and money paid for services to developers produced null and void results, and a fresh attempt at data migration was started on Hopp with a business-led approach. Thus, I recommend avoiding the adventure of ETL tools and hiring database/ETL developers if the outcome of DMMA is pointing to the south.

Mind the Metadata

Regardless of the business-led or technology-led approach, while navigating the most cost-effective path that ensures smooth data migration on the decommissioning night, as a program or project manager, you should also evaluate the need and extent of capturing metadata generated by the data migration. This is covered in more detail in Chapter 5, Business Rules. Metadata of data migration mainly includes the choices and decisions made on and about legacy data, including business rules, mapping rules, data cleansing rules, and data transformations done to uplift data quality.

Smooth continuity of business operations is the primary measure of the success or failure of data migration and overall decommissioning efforts. However, decision support, A.K.A. operational or business intelligence team, could refer to the metadata generated by data migration for the next few years post-decommissioning for historical data aggregation needs.

In a technology-led approach, database (ETL) developers lead data migration and liaise with internal SMEs, technical and data teams, vendors, consultants, and the project team. With this approach, remember the documentation, as you may risk losing knowledge about codified business rules for data migration (the metadata generated by data migration). Enforcing a Data Migration Plan and supporting documentation in a technology-led approach can ensure that the metadata generated by data migration is captured and saved for future reference. On the other hand, in the business-led approach, where data migration is a managed service from the vendor of the target system or a third-party consultant such as Hopp, the Data Migration Plan must be enforced here, too. However, the intensity of related documentation will vary depending on automated data lineage and documentation features of the data migration solution.

Questions to Ask

The third component of the plan, which focuses on people and technology, is crucial for resource planning. Its depth of information will vary depending on the project's current state, such as the selection of a target system and whether the level of vendor support is known or not. Overall, this component should answer the following questions:

- Which specific tools and personnel are essential for executing a successful data migration?

- Does the vendor provide managed services for data migration?

- Can we use our current Extract, Transform, and Load (ETL) solution and resources for the data discovery and transformation processes, considering the potential cost and time savings?

- Which toolset should we choose for ETL, such as SSIS, Informatica, Python, etc?

- Shall we host the data migration solution on-premises or in the cloud?

- What are the licensing cost and consulting costs for data migration tools?

- When was the last time a data management maturity assessment was done, and what was the outcome?

- As a part of project preparation, shall we undertake a professional data management maturity assessment?

- Have we evaluated the availability and skillsets of SMEs and technical team members to support data migration?

- Should we onboard specialist consultants and end-to-end data migration software to manage data migration professionally?

- What is the risk and possible impact due to limited in-house resource availability for data migration?

- How could we ensure that all information/metadata generated during data migration, such as decisions made and business rules defined, is captured for future reference?

CHAPTER 5

Business Rules

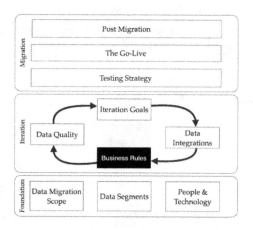

While the first three components of the data migration framework set the foundation before a single piece of code is written for data migration, we now focus on the actual operational nuances of moving the legacy data into the new target system. From here, we enter the "Iteration" stage of the data migration project, where business rules take center stage, guiding the entire data transformation process and code that ensures the integrity of the migrated data in the target system.

> *A business rule* is nothing, but every decision made about legacy data to perform data migration, starting with the data migration scope in the foundational stage to defining mappings between source and target data structures during the iteration stage.

DMBOK identifies collecting business rules as a critical activity for the data integration stream, including data migration. According to DMBOK, a business rule is a statement that defines or constrains an aspect of business processing while asserting the business structure and influencing the business's behavior [17]. Hence, I consider "business rules" as a standalone component of the framework that informs stakeholders about how business rules are validated and how business knowledge is retained for future needs.

What is an Iteration?

In the data migration context, an iteration refers to one data migration test run cycle that discovers gaps and issues as if you are executing an actual data migration today. An iteration begins with preparing the source system for data extraction, extracting the legacy data, transforming it to fit the target data structure, and loading the transformed legacy data in the new system. An iteration is logically successful if end users can execute business operations in the new system with the legacy data migrated in that iteration. If you can scope out each iteration and define success criteria for an iteration before its execution, you can measure the progression of the data migration project after each iteration.

During an iteration, you could find issues and limitations at any stage of the journey with repercussions on one or more stages of the iteration. For example, after migrating employee master data in the new payroll system, you find UI/UX issues in employee registration screens when updating the phone numbers of existing employees migrated from the legacy system. The root cause is the employee's mandatory team allocation ID, which is missing in the backend.

In this case, if the number of teams is small (< 100), you could manually load team master data in the target system to generate team IDs and map them with legacy team IDs in the next iteration. At the same time, the vendor must ensure that the attribute Teams ID is mandatory in the data upload template for employees. Being mandatory at the load stage, legacy employee data without TeamID cannot make it to the UI/UX (or UAT) testing and is parked for further investigation for the next iteration.

For the first iteration, start small with one or two logical master datasets (patient, customer, wards, beds, store locations, etc.) and limited, temporary, or placeholder business rules. Subsequently, as the scope widens, the frequency of approving, adding, and modifying business rules intensifies with discoveries in each iteration until there is no issue or gap in data migration. It's worth noting that your ETL solution or specialized data migration tool must be scalable to handle iterative enhancements and changes to the data flow and underneath code while keeping a log of all data rejections.

Mapping = Business Rules

Data migration is about meaningfully moving data from one structure to another, preserving its integrity, context, and usability. Therefore, it requires well-analyzed and validated mappings of data entities (tables, attributes, or fields) in the target system to those in the source (legacy) system [18] [19]. In the last chapter, we learned that the target system's data structure could be tables and columns in an actual SQL database, a bunch of Excel files (as templates), or REST API endpoints to push legacy data into the new system. Whatever the means on the target side, each attribute/field/column of the target table/Excel/APIs must be mapped with the legacy data structure.

Mapping decisions made for data migration directly impact business continuity post-decommissioning of the legacy system. Therefore, I see each data migration decision as a business decision that must be reviewed, approved, and documented as a data migration business rule. Trivial choices, such as using any default values (UNK, Unknown, or None) for a target attribute or leaving something NULL, are also part of mapping and, thus, a business rule.

DMBOK defines mapping as a synonym for transformation that addresses both the process of developing the lookup matrix from source to target structure and the result of that process. "A mapping defines the source to be extracted, the rules for identifying data for extraction, targets to be loaded, rules for identifying target rows for the update, and any transformation rules or calculations to be applied." In some cases (especially master data), this mapping could be simple with a one-to-one match between the source and target system (for example, customer first name).

However, mapping could get complex when the target data structure demands that the value be derived or transformed from one or multiple attributes (of one or multiple tables) of the source system. On the other hand, reference data (such as Gender and Product Type) would differ between legacy and target systems, requiring a lookup structure to derive the correct target value from the source value (e.g., M in the source is MALE in the target).

You can also come across some mandatory fields/columns in the target system that are unavailable in the years-old legacy system, leading to a hardcoded default value for the migrated data. Tables 2 and 3 show highly simplified examples of capturing mapping between source and target data structures for a few target fields/columns when migrating patient data. SMEs should review and validate such mapping before database developers can implement it in the ETL code.

Target Field	Mapping-Table(s)andField(s)	Mapping Type	Rules
medical_record _number	pt_master.pt_code	one-to-one	Mustbeuniqueforonepatient.
			DiscardInvalid,NULLanddummyp atientswithnon-numericvalueinpt_code
creation_date_t ime	pt_master.pt_last_refr esh_date.	one-to-one	SetNULLto'1753-01-01'
sex_rcd	pt_master.gender_typ e	one-to-one	Convert'I'orNULLto'U'
title_rcd	pt_master.title.ApplyF ollowingRules	one-to-one	StartingWith=Mappedto
			BR'='BROTHER'
			DR'or'DOCT'='DOCTOR'
			DAME'='DAME'
			FR'or'FATH'or'FATR'or'FTHR'='F ATHER'
			LAD'='LADY'
			BAB'or'MAST'='MASTER'
			MIS'='MISS'
			MR'='MISTER'
			MRS'='MRS';
			MS'='MS';
			PROF'='PROFESSOR'
			REV'='REVEREND'
			SIR'='SIR'
			STR'or'SIST'or'ST'or'STR'or'SIS R'or'STR'='SISTER'
			Everythingelse,SettoNULL
first_name	pt_master.first_given_ name	one-to-one	

Target Field	Mapping-Table(s)andField(s)	Mapping Type	Rules
last_name	pt_master.last_given_name	one-to-one	
common_name	pt_name.preferred_name_ind	derived	If pt_names.preferred_name_ind=1then Merge second_given_name and third_givern_name to compose the common_name Else if preffered_name_ind = 2 then use second_given_name Else for all other cases use third_given_name
	pt_master.third_given_name		
	pt_master.second_given_name		
mainden_name	Data not available in the legacy system	none	
mothers_maiden_name	Data not available in the legacy system	none	

Table 2: Business Rules First Example

Target Field	Mapping-Table(s)andField(s)	Mapping Type	Rules
occupation_rcd	pt_master.occp_code and tbl_occupations.occp_description	lookup-map	Mapping file under development. Set to 9999-Unknown temporary
occupation_status_rcd	Data not available in the legacy system	none	
residence_country_rcd	pt_master.cry_code	lookup-map	Use mapping file source_country_code_mapping.csv - Report outliers and map them to UNK.
religion_rcd	pt_master.rgl_code	one-to-one	MappingRequired
date_of_birth	pt_master.birth_date	one-to-one	
birth_place	pt_master.pob_descr	one-to-one	

Target Field	Mapping-Table(s)andField(s)	Mapping Type	Rules
country_of_birth_rcd	pt_master.pob_country_code	lookup-map	Use mapping file source_country_code_mapping.csv - Report outliers and map them to UNK.
date_of_death	pt_master.death_date	one-to-one	
passport_number	Data not available in the legacy system	none	
smoker_rcd	pt_master.smoker_ind	lookup-code	Map Y to'CS',N to'NS','U' and NULL to'UNK'.
smoker_comment	Data not available in the legacy system	none	
drug_usage_rcd	Data not available in the legacy system	none	Setto'UNK'
drug_usage_comment	Data not available in the legacy system	none	
patient_allergy_status_rcd	pt_master._pt_code allergies_master.pt_code	derived	True if pt_code exists in the allergies_master table. Else false

Table 3: Business Rules Second Example

Whether complex or simple, the mapping between source and target data structure is a bunch of business rules that control data transformation from source to target system. A business could need these business rules retrospectively post-decommission for various analytical or compliance needs. Thus, it must be captured, curated, and approved by SMEs or stakeholders and made available in a human-readable form. Poorly executed data migration, where the mapping between source and target structure was considered as purely a technical job, would bury all such business rules in the data transformation code without any scrutiny for transform logic or default values for the mandatory fields, causing significant risk in meeting analytical needs and disrupting downstream data feeds to integrated systems.

The rules that map the target data structure with the source data structure (the legacy system) to transform or cleanse the data during migration, de-duplicate rules, etc., must be explicitly validated and documented as business knowledge. Documenting business rules for such a significant transition would add value as metadata generated from the data migration and serve as a reliable reference for future analytical or regulatory needs that demand data aggregation from the legacy and current systems. When buried in data transformation code (and in the developer's head, who no longer works here), legacy and current data aggregation would depend on a massive reverse-engineering exercise, causing doubts about the integrity of the combined dataset. Therefore, the value of your work in documenting these business rules cannot be overstated.

Please refrain from attempting to list all business rules in the plan, as they will emerge and develop as the data migration project progresses. Instead, focus on including information about how business rules are validated, who (SMEs) are responsible for the validation, and provide a reference to the location where business rules are documented. Depending on the culture, budget, and preferences, one can capture business rules in a simple Excel file saved in SharePoint or opt for a sophisticated business rule engine that allows non-technical users to manage business rules.

As Data Migration Lead in my first project, I used to build mapping files with business rules in an Excel sheet, which I can use in my brief dedicated time with SMEs to run through them over my proposed mapping for their validation. It was always a productive exercise with two to three rounds per Excel sheet that ensured comprehensive business rule gathering and well-structured ETL code and data pipelines that execute those business rules on the legacy data. The data migration process and underlying ETL code gained trust due to thorough SME validation of business rules.

In my most successful data migration, I analyzed every attribute of the data upload templates provided by the vendor. For each target attribute, I captured information about how data is populated during data migration. In hindsight, having business rules validated by SMEs for each target attribute did not eliminate all issues and surprises during test runs. However, it established a process to raise and prioritize new issues for timely resolution or business rule formation, eventually leading to successful data migration on the go-live night.

We will see how this simple and fine-grained approach to business rules validation assisted me in measuring data migration progress in Chapter 8, Iteration Goals.

> *The key point to note here is to analyze every target attribute and generate one spreadsheet file with business rules for each target dataset.*

These files should be a project deliverable and part of the project files, along with the data migration plan that points to locations and names of files with business rules. You will thank me later when your decision support and other data analyst tribes utilize this comprehensive and validated documentation multiple times after the go live.

Questions to Ask

Leverage the fourth component of the data migration framework to create a process for curating and capturing critical business knowledge generated due to the decommissioning of the legacy system and decisions made on legacy data during data migration. Overall, this component should answer the following questions:

- Are we migrating all critical data elements in the legacy system into the new system for regulatory, financial, and operational needs?

- How are we handling mandatory data in the target system that is unavailable in the source system?

- What is the process for defining and validating mapping between source and target as business rules?

- What is the process for finding information about how we migrated legacy data after the decommissioning?

- What are the criteria to select the correct customer /product/ patient (master data) when duplicates are found within one legacy system or between multiple instances of the legacy systems?

CHAPTER 6

Data Quality

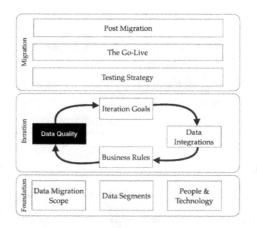

Gartner reports that data migration projects frequently surpass their budgets by 25% to 100% or more, primarily due to insufficient proactive management of data quality issues. According to the Data Management Body of Knowledge (DMBOK), data quality refers to the characteristics of high-quality data and the processes used to measure or improve data quality [20]. Having delved into the first four components of the data migration framework, we now focus on the elephant in the room: data quality.

We will first analyze the potential characteristics of legacy data that should be deemed high-quality for data migration and later review the quality controls for measuring and improving data quality over multiple iterations. I am not exaggerating when I say that poor data quality in a legacy system could single-handedly hamper your budgets and plans for data migration. In this chapter, we will explore the significance of data quality and the repercussions of poor data quality in the legacy system on data migration progress and business continuity post-migration.

> *The quality of anything (clothes, car, pen, air, any object) matters when you consume or use it. Therefore, the quality of legacy data matters when it is used to initiate a new business system with existing business data.*

For a successful data migration project, one must clearly define the characteristics of high-quality data to be deemed as fit-for-purpose and what processes and measures will ensure the highest possible data quality in the migrated data.

Poor/bad quality of legacy data invites three significant risks:

- The target system completely rejects a significant subset of the legacy data.
- Poor quality data enters the target system and disturbs the user interface and business processes.

- Poor quality data enters the target system and disturbs downstream data integration and reporting.

In any data migration project, prioritizing the highest possible quality of the legacy data in the new business system is crucial. Therefore, the data migration plan must comprehensively address the current state of data quality and the strategies deployed to enhance the legacy data's suitability for the new system.

Fit-for-Migration = Good Quality

The widely used data quality dimensions (Completeness, Uniqueness, Timeliness, Validity, Accuracy, and Consistency) can be a sound choice to assess and describe the state of quality of the legacy data within the scope of migration [21] [22] [23]. While this dimension-based data quality assessment is the best method to determine the data quality before a statistical or analytical use case, utilizing all six dimensions to denote fit-for-migration data across the legacy system can be overcooked in tight timeframes and budgets. In the same breath, I also want to emphasize that data migration is your golden opportunity to improve the overall data quality of the business data and establish standards and KPIs for data quality in the new system with enhanced business processes.

For data migration purposes, legacy data is of high quality if it does not violate any constraints enforced by the target data structure and conforms to all data quality audit checks before the upload. I loosely grouped these checks and constraints into two types of characteristics of high-quality data for migration: validity and integrity. For example, only letters are accepted for a customer name; only digits in pin-code or gender_code must be "M," "F," or "U," which are data validity checks. In contrast, rejecting an order record from migration because the customer it belongs to is missing from the customer data ensures transactional integrity.

The following are some examples of data quality rules. The first four examples define the validity of the data in terms of the semantics of individual values. In contrast, other rules denote data integrity due to the inherent relationship between master and transactional datasets within the scope of migration.

Examples of data validity rules:

- Customer Name must have A-Z or a-z and space only.
- Phone number must have digits between 0–9 only.
- Customer Date of birth must be less than the current date.
- Order Date must be a valid date in 'YYYY-MM-DD' format.

Examples of data integrity rules:

- Product and customer data must exist to accept an order record from that customer, which includes products.
- Patient data must exist to accept a referral record for that patient.

- A referral must exist to create an appointment or waiting-list record for that particular referral.

The physical data model of the target data structure can enforce data validity and integrity constraints. You must achieve this bare minimum data quality to load extracted and transformed legacy data into the target system. Whereas some constraints for data validity and integrity can be business-process driven and not always coded as constraints in the physical data model, its violations can pose a significant risk of causing user experience (UX) issues in the new target system, potentially leaving users with incomplete business processes and an invalid system of record. For example, the new patient management system cannot process migrated patient appointments due to missing referral information, which was not migrated with the appointments.

Therefore, a robust data quality audit to assess business-process-driven constraints (a.k.a., business rules) on the final staged data for migration is critical to reject invalid data. Check with your vendor about their process for such data quality audit, which can be as basic as custom SQL procedures to sophisticated business preload validations available in SAP, where an artifact called preload files are generated from staged data to represent how the data will appear in the SAP system and ensure the data meets all business rules [24].

Reject invalid data from the migration (with succinct log) that fails checks or violates any constraint and aim to achieve the highest possible throughput for the clean staged data. To achieve this, data quality audits and constraints in the target database should flow into the data transformation code—the T of the ETL. During the data transformation, identify and reject low-quality data from migration for rectification in the source system and implement automation for data cleansing where possible.

Imagine filling a new city reservoir with water from an old, contaminated source. Without filtration and quality checks, the polluted water would flow through every tap in the city, affecting thousands. Now, substitute "water" with "data" and "city" with your new business system. Migrating bad data without cleansing is like distributing contaminated water—it will poison decision-making, customer service, and compliance.

This is why data quality must be assessed, monitored, and enhanced before, during, and after migration.

Please be aware that text fields for phone numbers and addresses in legacy systems are the deathbed of data quality expectations that demand significant time to develop and test data cleansing code. Secondly, intelligent people in your organization may have invented new ways within their team or department of utilizing one or more attributes on the UI of a static legacy system not modified over the years. Such innovative and diverse ways of data entry can prove costly as permanent data-quality leakage. To achieve high-quality data migration, you will need your people to change their data-entry habits on the legacy system and people leaders to rise to their responsibilities to ensure high-quality data is entered into the legacy system.

Continuous Monitoring

Unlike a legacy system-built decades ago, a newer business system will likely have more coherent and sophisticated data quality/integrity checks enforced in the physical data model and user interface as business rules. Therefore, preparing a list of all data quality checks in the target system from early on, and accommodating these checks in the data migration code to flag invalid data will set up a foundation to identify, measure, and rectify poor data quality issues before they can cause unexpected behavior in the new system or halt the whole migration.

A data quality report with a list of the problems and the number of records affected must be produced and shared with stakeholders to allocate ownership of manual data cleansing and identify low-hanging issues remediable by programming. New issues are expected to surface with each data migration test run. However, the number of rejected records due to poor data quality should eventually decline with continuous test runs, with the highest possible data quality achieved before decommissioning. I used to engage stakeholders with data storytelling thanks to the enriched information captured during each test run about the state of data quality. I would further map invalid data back to the team who entered it to set ownership for manual cleansing and monitor teams who needs data-entry training refresher.

A simple example of data quality reporting and data visualization to monitor and communicate the state of the data quality are below.

Target Template	Data Quality Issue	Record Count
Patient	Failed country of birth validation	230
Patient	Failed patient identifiers validation.	432
Patient	Failed phone number validation.	100
Patient Address	Failed Address1 validation.	125
Patient Address	Filed pin code validation.	345
Patient Contacts and Relatives	Failed name validation.	568
Patient Contacts and Relatives	Failed phone number validation.	435
Patient Alias Names	Failed name validation.	256
Outpatient Appointments	Appointment date is more than 20 years in the past	12
Outpatient Appointments	Appointment date is more than 10 years in the future.	34
Inpatient Visits	mandatory bed code missing or invalid.	457
Inpatient Visits	sugery_date is mandatory.	66
Inpatient Visits	primary_provider_team is mandatory.	345

Table 4: Data Quality Reporting Example

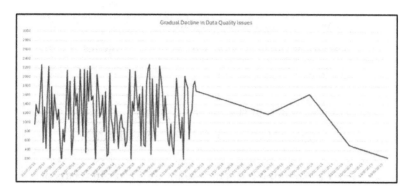

Figure 4: Monitor and Communicate Data Quality and Data Cleansing Efforts

Proactive data quality measurement with good data governance practices can significantly reduce the time and effort to prepare legacy data fit-for-migration. However, in worst cases with no formal data quality and governance practices, a legacy decommissioning project can bring the golden opportunity to do things right in terms of improvising data-entry practices and uplifting overall data quality of the legacy system in preparation for decommissioning and continuous monitoring of exemplary data-quality practices in the new business system as well.

Questions to Ask

Leverage the fifth component of the data migration framework to assess, measure, and monitor the quality of the legacy data. This component addresses the following questions of stakeholders:

- What is the state of data quality in the legacy system, and what are the current data quality standards/practices?

- How do we measure the quality of legacy data to ensure it is fit for purpose, and who is responsible for the high quality of legacy data?

- Does the current state of data quality negatively impact the fitness of the legacy data for migration?

- Is this the opportunity to do things better in terms of monitoring data quality in the legacy system?

- How would we ensure that invalid data does not disrupt the new system or downstream integration for data warehousing and reporting?

- Which data quality enforcement/standards are implemented in the target system?

- Are data quality and integrity audits in place by the vendor before migrating legacy data into the new system?

- How should we measure data quality and form a roadmap for gradual improvements?

- How can manual and automated data cleansing efforts be efficiently planned?

CHAPTER 7

Data Integrations

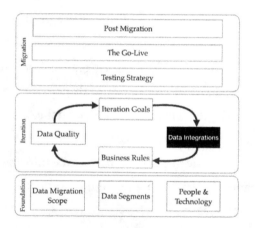

A standalone system without any downstream or upstream data integrations is as rare as finding a giraffe in the desert.

A critical business system integrates with other internal or external systems through synchronous or asynchronous methods.

Secondly, essential business systems at the core of business operations supply data into a data analytics or business intelligence platform, such as a data warehouse or contemporary data lake house, to meet operational and management reporting needs [25]. Hence, the migration plan must assess the impact of data migration on the existing data integration dependencies on the legacy system. This chapter will address the factors to consider in data migration to minimize the risk of interruptions in downstream or upstream data integration.

A new modern system replacing the legacy system would differ significantly in the depth and scope of features it can support compared to older systems built decades ago. It may bring new system integration capabilities that are unavailable in the legacy system or include many operational reports and out-of-the-box analytics currently powered by centralized data warehouse and reporting teams [26]. Therefore, it is essential to assess the current state of data integration interfaces in the legacy system, as well as the capabilities of the target system, to make informed choices for data migration, meriting a standalone component in the data migration framework.

I once witnessed a situation where the legacy patient management system in public hospitals provided various data extracts to the centralized national data warehouse for almost a decade for national statistics and reporting on the utilization and demand of emergency, inpatient, and outpatient services. Some extracts were snapshots, whereas a few captured continuous journeys of a care episode that started with accepting a GP referral for the patient, which could result in inpatient and outpatient visits spanning a period. With post-discharge annual visits, an episode of care can also last for multiple years. Missing this data integration dependency while retiring the legacy patient management system caused significant delays and costs post-legacy decommissioning in re-establishing the continuous supply of data extracts for national reporting from the new patient management system. Another example was the inability to integrate the latest patient management system with the theatre management system due to a single missing field in the APIs of the new patient management system, which resulted in a costly product enhancement request.

Decisions regarding refactoring or retiring any existing integration of the legacy system to accommodate the new system are outside the scope of this chapter. However, business rules for data transformation during the data migration can directly impact upstream and downstream data integrations. Therefore, this component of the data migration framework emphasizes engaging with internal data management teams and experts early on in the data migration process to gather all potential risks and possible mitigation approaches. You can further narrow your analysis into two use cases: system integration and data extraction.

System Integration

The core consideration here is the open business processes that will be completed with related data captured in the new system after the day of decommissioning. For example, an inpatient with all his information captured in the legacy system will be discharged after three days when the new patient management system is live, changing how discharge data is supplied to downstream integrations. Similarly, a bulk of orders received in the legacy system will be shipped when the new system is in place. Business rules formations and resulting data transformations must factor in open business processes in the legacy system and the impact of choices made on integration dependencies and business continuity.

Supporting existing system integrations of the legacy system with the new system can enforce some restrictions on data transformation during migration, which must be discovered early on in the project and raised promptly with the vendor of the new system. When decommissioning a legacy system, poorly planned data migration poses a significant risk of corrupting downstream data integration and interrupting business process execution. For example, a business-critical integration, dependent on the legacy system's alphanumeric field, cannot continue because the equivalent field is a numeric attribute in the new system. In this example, either the integration interface or the target data structure needs some tweaks, subject to a thorough cost-benefit analysis to determine the best choice.

I recall my experience of last-minute changes in the logic of a derived unique identifier for a patient visit, based initially on the concatenation of the legacy referral number and visit timestamp. During system integration testing, when the patient is discharged from the hospital, the visit identifier flows into downstream invoicing systems that try to extract the patient number from it. A choice made for data migration turned into a showstopper that would have caused a lot of trouble in production if it had gone unnoticed. Therefore, before you finalize any business rules for target attributes, gather all possible documentation on the existing integration interface design and determine which attributes/fields of the legacy data, in what format, are essential for an integrated data flow to work.

Raise showstoppers early to avoid disappointments later and give your stakeholders enough time to analyze and find potential solutions.

Data Extraction

A large enterprise will likely have a data warehouse accepting data feeds from the legacy system over the years, where data is modeled and arranged in some dimensional model. The new business systems can introduce changes in data types or semantics of unique identifiers of significant business entities that directly impact existing data warehouses and analytical data marts. On the other hand, the new system may meet most or all operational reporting needs, demanding the retirement of numerous centralized reports. Therefore, replacing a legacy system will open the opportunity to optimize data extraction needs to support existing data warehouse and reporting solutions.

Let me warn you that if your organization has recently invested millions in getting an excellent data warehouse up and running with your legacy system as a predominant data source, some data people can appear upset for no reason throughout the lifecycle of the data migration project. I don't blame them. If I were on their end, I would be disappointed with the retirement of the legacy system, too. Data warehouses and data marts are not built overnight or over a week. Discontinuing data feeds from the legacy system and switching to the new system as the data source for the data warehouse would require substantial analysis and development work with robust testing.

As an employee for an organization with such a significant change, you also have the opportunity to assess your existing reporting and data warehousing needs due to inbuilt operational and analytical reports in the target system. I observed that legacy system performance issues and (or) skyrocketing customization costs push operational reporting out of the enterprise data warehouse in large organizations. You don't necessarily need all existing operational reports or to maintain all fact and dimension tables in the data warehouse when the new system is up and running. Analysis of data models and business keys of a current data warehouse is essential to make sound choices when forming business rules for data migration.

Questions to Ask

Leverage the sixth component of the data migration framework to assess, control, and ensure uninterrupted upstream and downstream data integration and, eventually, business continuity. The component addresses the following questions of stakeholders:

- Do we have a data warehouse for reporting with data feeds from the legacy system?

- Have we evaluated the impact of data migration on the existing data integrations?

- Have we gathered and evaluated downstream integration requirements?

- Do we have a list of must-haves, should, and could-have classifications of desired integration?

- How do we manage post-go-live continuity for operational and management reporting?

- How will we meet critical operational reporting required from day one post-go-live?

- Who should take risk ownership for uninterrupted data integration—the BAU data management team or the project team?

- What are the estimated refactoring efforts in terms of time and cost to upgrade data warehouse processes and data models to accept data from the new system?

CHAPTER 8

Iteration Goals

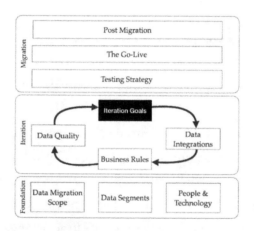

One of the reputed researchers in Change Management, John P. Kotter, articulated eight reasons why organizations fail to execute change. In this list, number 6 is "Failing to create Short-Term Wins," emphasizing the necessity of early and regular feedback on success. I want to express the significance of iteration goals by quoting the following paragraph from the Change Management chapter in the DMBOK [27]: *"Complex change efforts require*

short-term goals in support of long-term objectives. Meeting these goals allows the team to celebrate and maintain momentum. The key thing is to create the short-term win rather merely hoping for it. In successful transformations, managers actively establish early goals, achieve thesis goals, and reward the team. Without systematic efforts to guarantee success, change is likely to fail."

Ignoring data migration test iterations and assuming that legacy data is fit for migration on the cutover day is like catching a flying lizard with your mouth wide open—not a good idea that indeed invites trouble.

In the first six components of the data migration framework, we identified all the ingredients necessary to cook a palatable data migration dish when replacing a legacy business application. However, from determining the ingredients to cooking the final dish for the big day is a prolonged process that requires several test migration runs before the big day, usually called the cutover, decommissioning, or go-live day. As a program/project manager or business stakeholder, data migration test iterations are your opportunity to assess how close you are to achieving a smooth data migration if it were to be executed today.

Over multiple test iterations, we (the project team and vendor) realize whether data migration is working or not as expected and how long it takes to complete the end-to-end migration process, from switching off (or freezing) the legacy system, migrating data, conducting smoke tests, and finally switching on the new system for business transactions. Executing multiple test runs before the cutover is recommended to prepare and ensure robust and frictionless migration on the cutover day. The logic behind test-runs is to identify gaps in the legacy data to make it fit for migration by facilitating necessary data mapping, transformation, and cleansing activities before the cutover.

For an extensive business system, we can safely assume that it is never ready to be used straight out of the box and requires customization to meet the functional and non-functional needs of the business. This customization often occurs while data migration activities happen in the background. With a timeworn legacy system as the source and the target system under customization, the data migration project faces the dilemma of an unknown source and a moving target. In such cases, data migration iterations are crucial to identify gaps in the business's readiness to switch to the new system.

Leaving the test runs purely as technical tasks that move data from location A to B and are handled by internal database analysts/developers and the new system vendor, can lead to unforeseen issues on the cutover day or post-migration due to overlooked dependencies.

Addressing and planning what you want to achieve from each test iteration is vital, as this will bring the business one step closer to a successful data migration on cutover day with minimized risk.

From one iteration to the next, you will discover new data quality issues, gaps in mapping, downstream integration showstoppers and the introduction of new target attributes, which will result in new business rules. Tracking what has been achieved so far and what is left for the next iteration is essential to measuring and minimizing the risk of data migration and setting tangible goals for the next iteration. Thus, deserving a dedicated component in the framework and a chapter that sheds light on measuring and planning test iterations for data migration.

Measure, Communicate, and Iterate

In the second component of the data migration framework, we examined the logical segments of data and the migration order—specifically, master and transactional data. In the initial test runs, I highly recommend migrating master data and conducting brief UI/UX testing of the new system with the migrated data. Many key challenges will likely surface immediately, even with just master data in the scope of migration test runs. These challenges are addressed early on, and processes defined to manage showstoppers (issues) will speed up the migration work when you start migrating transactional data.

Data Migration Templates	Migration Status	Extract	Transform	Load	Loaded in UAT	Tested in UAT
Workforce						
Medical Proffesionals	100%	100%	100%	100%	100%	N
Teams	0%	0%	0%	0%	0%	N
Team Members	0%	0%	0%	0%	0%	N
Patient Management System						
Admission Requests	98%	95%	100%	95%	100%	N
Appointments	88%	87%	76%	76%	100%	N
Inpatient Visits	89%	85%	83%	83%	100%	N
Outpaitient Visits	93%	93%	88%	88%	100%	N
Inpatient Transfers	0%	0%	0%	0%	0%	N
Inpatient Caregivers	85%	78%	78%	78%	100%	N
Inpatient Discharged	92%	92%	83%	75%	100%	N
Inpatient Leaves	67%	100%	100%	100%	0%	N
Patient Address	100%	100%	100%	100%	100%	Y
Patient Alias Names	100%	100%	100%	100%	100%	N
Patient Contacts	100%	100%	100%	100%	100%	N
Patient Legal Status	100%	100%	100%	100%	100%	N
Patient Providers	100%	100%	100%	100%	100%	N
Referrals	92%	89%	87%	87%	100%	N
Referral Priority	100%	100%	100%	100%	100%	N
Referrals Funder	100%	100%	100%	100%	100%	N
Inpatient Medical Codes	100%	100%	100%	100%	99%	Y
Patients	100%	100%	100%	100%	100%	N
Service providers	96%	100%	100%	100%	89%	N
Referral Medical Coding	88%	82%	82%	82%	100%	N
Waiting List	85%	78%	78%	77%	100%	N
Emergency Visits	60%	90%	90%	80%	0%	N
Emergency Triages	67%	100%	100%	100%	0%	N
Medical Record Folders	0%	0%	0%	0%	0%	N

Total percentage done   77%

Table 5: Data Migration Status Dashboard - Patient Management System

One key challenge in migrating master data is mapping the reference data between the legacy and new systems, such as gender codes, country codes, customer types, or product types. On the other hand, complex mappings that require business approval can delay your test runs indefinitely. In such cases, map everything to a default value in the target system, such as 'UNKNOWN', 'UNK', or NULL, to push data with minimal effort. The idea is to migrate as much data as possible using temporary placeholders for attributes that need further analysis and business approval. With each iteration, the temporary placeholders for data attributes should decrease as all mapping rules are documented in the Business Rule component of the plan. Some business rules may take a long time to approve, but this should not delay the migration of data attributes that are ready for migration. I remember how it took me forever to map the location codes of wards and rooms in the hospital to new hierarchical location identifiers in the target system. The delay was not technical; preparing and approving a hierarchical location map of all wards and rooms across all public hospitals took a while.

The conventional way to measure data migration success is by comparing the number of records extracted from the source system to those migrated into the target system. However, more is needed to provide a complete picture. For example, we could migrate millions of customers or patient records with only the first and last names, while all other attributes or fields are defaulted to NULL or UNKNOWN.

How exactly can we measure data migration progress?

If you choose a data migration tool such as Hopp or engage a specialist consultant, check their solutions and ideas to measure data migration progress. For now, let me share my tactics. During my first data migration project as the "Data Migration Lead," I faced the challenge of measuring and reporting data migration progress to the steering committee, which included senior business stakeholders and executives. In 2015–16, I developed a simple method using an Excel file.

We never migrate data directly into the backend of the target system, which consists of hundreds of tables. Instead, the target system uses intermediary data upload mechanisms such as CSV/Excel data templates, denormalized SQL tables in a staging database, or REST APIs with POST calls. Let's collectively call these mechanisms "upload templates," which come with documentation (from the vendor) explaining each data attribute of the template (such as a data dictionary). Depending on the complexity of the target system, its vendor may provide 20 to 50 such upload templates that need to be filled with transformed legacy data, ready to be uploaded into the target system.

For each field/attribute in an upload template, mark four actions with a Boolean flag (1/0) to consider the field successfully migrated if all flags are 1. These four actions for a single target attribute are Mapped, Business Rule Defined, Data Quality

Target Attribute	Mapped	Business Rule	Data Quality	Loaded	Completion
Patient Name	1	1	1	1	1
Appointment Date	1	0	1	1	0
Appointment Time	1	0	1	1	0
Appointment Outcome	1	1	1	1	1
...					
Completed %					50%

Table 6: Data Migration Progress - At a Template Level

Verified, and Loaded in the Target. Not all target attributes of an upload template will require all four actions. In such cases, flag the non-required action as 1 (Done). For an upload template (to migrate appointment data) with 60 attributes/fields, if 25 are marked as completed with all four flags set to 1, the data migration progress for the template is 41.67%.

It took me a few hours to prepare the first Excel file with three tabs for three upload templates, initially marking most fields as Zero. Updating Zeros with Ones (One with Zero sometimes) for Mapped, Business Rule, and Data Quality flags, was part of my regular work routine whenever I developed or changed ETL code for any target attribute. After the test run, I set the Loaded flag to 1 for an attribute if the target system accepts all the data for that attribute and no UI/UX issues are detected during the testing. I gradually scaled it to display the completion percentage for all upload templates (Shown above in Image 9). On the dashboard tab, five fields at the attribute level are simplified as average in three columns: Extract (Mapped), Transform (Data Quality and Business Rule), and Load (Loaded and Completion). As you would have guessed, the final Migration Status "77%" is the average of the Extract, Transform, and Load columns. Loaded in UAT and Tested in UAT can be added later with the formal commencement of the UAT testing.

After some initial heavy lifting, it was a relatively simple task to change flags with the progress in data migration code development, identify new issues, and introduce new columns every fortnight due to customizations in the target system. With this approach, I kept an up-to-date data migration status report for the business stakeholders after each fortnightly migration test run. With clear visibility of bottlenecks, stakeholders could push the right levers to remove or find a solution around any showstoppers in data migration activities.

During the project, customizations in the target system introduced new upload templates and altered the existing one every fortnight for over two years, which caused variations in the data migration completion percentage every fortnight. However, as the code freeze came closer and the frequency of changes got smaller, the above method of reporting data migration progress helped to pinpoint individual target attributes with pending activities (mapping, business rule, data quality, loaded). After a few test runs, I could share the progression visually, locate flags with 0s, specify which action was missing, and highlight target attributes with prolonged delays from the stakeholders in business rules approvals.

Questions to Ask

Data migration test iterations are critical in minimizing the risk of data migration and measuring the gap between our current state and where we need to be. With each iteration, the project team should have means to quantify what is achieved and how much is left for the subsequent iterations.

Leverage this component of the data migration framework to plan test runs, attach objectives to test runs, and measure progress to orchestrate an uninterrupted data migration on the big cutover day. This component addresses the following questions from stakeholders:

- How frequently are trial migrations scheduled before the cutover?

- Have we defined the measures to track data migration progress with each trial run?

- How do we identify showstoppers or blockers preventing successful data migration?

CHAPTER 9

Testing Strategy

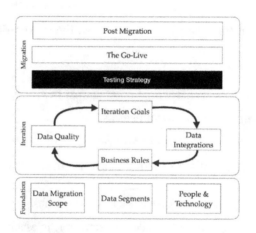

We are now in the third group, consisting of three components. In the last chapter, I covered the significance of planning multiple data migration test iterations before the actual go-live with the new business application. Let's look at what we need to test in each iteration and what our testing strategy could be to eliminate all unpleasant surprises stemming from the data migration process. Testing instills trust and confidence in the end-to-end data migration process. Improvising testing capabilities with each test iteration of data migration should be the logical way to progress and gradually improve the data migration success ratio with each test iteration.

Data migrating testing is a feedback loop, not a checkbox.

Many organizations treat testing as a one-time validation step rather than a continuous feedback loop. In reality, every migration test iteration should be analyze→ refine→ retest→ improve. Think of it as sculpting a statue—you don't carve everything in one go; you chisel, refine, step back, and adjust. Every iteration of testing should:

- Validate transformed data against business rules
- Simulate real-world use cases
- Capture mismatches and refine mapping
- Repeat until confidence is achieved.

Skipping testing iterations is like releasing a half-finished product into the market—it will break. Therefore, it is essential to foresee and mitigate any potential problems or glitches that could occur during or after the data migration. Thus, I place the testing strategy as a critical part of the data migration framework, which must be articulated in the data migration plan. I recommend a testing strategy covering three types of testing to ensure the best possible data migration:

- Data unit testing
- Data integrity testing
- Functional testing.

Data Unit Testing

By data unit testing, I refer to validating the data migration process for specific data sets (often referred to as business entities) through individual upload templates. The name is inspired by the traditional unit testing associated with testing each unit of function within a computer program. The data unit refers to each data upload template or logical data segment such as customer, patient, or customer address. Thus, Unit testing refers to testing data extraction and transforming logic for each upload template in isolation. Unit testing ensures no data loss due to logical errors in the data migration code or orchestration of the ETL process.

Data unit testing requires a comprehensive audit trail for each step of the data migration for every staged dataset. For instance, when migrating patient or customer data, the unit test includes checking and comparing the numbers of records extracted, transformed, loaded, and rejected for the patient or customer entity. It is not always a one-to-one match due to merge and duplicate removal and data quality rejection. Through Data unit testing for all datasets in migration, the project team can ensure that no data loss can occur due to glitches in the data extraction and transformation code, especially in derived data attributes where the value is calculated during data transformation.

Data Segment / Upload Template	Extracted From System 1	Extracted From System 2	Duplicate Removed	Rejected Poor Quality Data	Total Loaded
Health Service Providers	8700	7545	7545	100	8600
Patient	91247	50092	9422	4555	131917
Patient Addresses	130087	76951	1788	230	208226
Patient Contacts	292665	150966	0	10	443582
Patient Referrals	7243	0	0	33	54630
Appointments	346673	162104	0	67	508771
Outpatient Visits	8180	15446	0	98	7498

Table 7: Data Migration Progress - At a Template Level

For example, the data migration code for migrating customers from the legacy system should generate audit trail information that "X records of customers are extracted from the legacy system, Y records are loaded in the target system, while Z records were rejected and grouped in one more data quality issues that caused the rejection (duplicates, invalid entries, etc.)."

The objectives of data unit testing are:

- Ensure the correct number of records are extracted and loaded, considering any merge, duplication, or data quality rejections.

- Monitor for discrepancies between the extracted and loaded data, highlighting where data fails to meet the quality standards.

- Track the total count of records processed, rejected, or merged, ensuring traceability for every transformation.

Data Integrity Testing

Data Integrity Testing is done on the final dataset prepared for the load stage after the transformation. Data integrity testing ensures that the relationships between business entities in the legacy data remain intact post-migration and the data is fit for migration. Data integrity testing will be conducted on the final dataset prepared for the migration by executing an audit script that runs through all integrity checks and highlights the data violating any mandatory condition. For large transformation projects, it is a reasonable expectation from the vendor to either provide such audit mechanics before the data is uploaded or provide the necessary information to build one data integrity audit script that conducts a series of checks on the final dataset prepared for the migration.

Integrity testing through audit scripts is a must before the final dataset is pushed into the target system because it ensures migrated data is coherent and contains all data points comprising a business transaction in the target system. A comprehensive audit script should also ensure that all mandatory attributes required by the UI of the target system are present in the final dataset for migration to prevent any unexpected errors in the target system during operational use. For example:

- No order record can be loaded in the target system without the customer record already available who placed the order.

- Similarly, no appointment or booking information can exist without the corresponding patient record.

- Employee records must have a valid Team Identifier of a team already created in the target system.

The objectives of data integrity testing are:

- Audit business rules and relationships between entities in the migrated data, confirming that all relational data points are aligned and accurate.

- Automated audit scripts are used to run consistency checks across the entire dataset and confirm data relationships before loading data into the target system.

- Ensure there are no orphaned records or incomplete relationships that could impact the functionality of the business application.

- Improve data accuracy by ensuring the integrity of transactional data across multiple years is intact in the new system.

- Ensure migrated data is highly accurate, integrated, complete, and trustworthy.

Functional Testing

Functional testing is where "the rubber hits the road." It verifies that the migrated data functions as expected within the context of the new system. It involves testing real-world use cases to confirm that legacy data interacts seamlessly with the new application without breaking existing processes. One key aspect of functional testing is processing open transactions that were migrated from the legacy system, such as discharging a patient who was admitted when the legacy system was operational or dispatching goods for a sales order captured in the legacy system. Another critical functional area to test is ensuring upstream and downstream integrations work in the target system with migrated data without glitches.

Functional testing of data migration can be combined with system integration and user acceptance testing, which are part of the test plan for deploying the new business application. The planning of functional data migration testing needs careful consideration. It needs a dedicated test environment and resources for testing with real-world data, which may have regulatory constraints preventing its use. Secondly, you can only test some migrated records out of the millions migrated. Thus, a relatively tiny number of records are to be selected as a random sample size for the functional testing to ensure 95% to 99% confidence in the testing.

Calculating the sample size for data migration testing requires balancing statistical confidence and practical feasibility. A common approach involves applying statistical methods, such as random sampling, to select a subset of records for validation. The formula for calculating sample size based on confidence level, margin of error, and population is a standard statistical methodology widely used in survey sampling. A frequent citation for this is "Cochran, W. G. (1977). Sampling Techniques (3rd ed.). John Wiley and Sons." This book discusses sampling methods, including finite population correction and calculating sample sizes [28]. For now, here's a general guideline:

1. **Determine Confidence Level and Margin of Error:**

   - Common confidence levels are 95% or 99%.
   - Typical margins of error range from 2% to 5%.

2. Use the Sampling Formula:

$$n = \frac{Z^2 \cdot p \cdot (1 - p)}{e^2}$$

The standard formula for sample size in a large population is:

- **n:** Sample size.
- **Z:** Z-score corresponds to the desired confidence level. 1.96 for 95% confidence and 2.58 for 99%. Larger Z-scores (higher confidence levels) result in larger sample

sizes, as greater precision and certainty require more data.

- **p:** Estimated proportion of the attribute in the population (Maximum sample size occurs at p=0.5).
- **e:** Margin of error (e.g., 0.05 for 5%).

3. Apply Correction for Small Populations:

If your population (N) is finite, adjust the sample size:

$$n_{adjusted} = \frac{n}{1 + \left(\frac{n-1}{N}\right)}$$

For example, for 100,000 patient medical records in the migration scope, assuming a 95% confidence level and 5% error margin:

- For a population size of 100,000 records, the calculated sample size without considering finite population correction is approximately 384. When adjusting for the finite population size, the sample size required is approximately 383.

- You need to test and compare 383 patient records out of 100,000 migrated to the new system to ensure successful data migration with a 95% confidence level and a 5% margin of error.

```
In [17]:  #Given Values
          Z = 1.96   # Z-score for 95% confidence level
          p = 0.5    # Estimated proportion
          e = 0.05   # Margin of error
          N = 100000  # Population size

          # Sample size without finite population correction
          n = (Z**2 * p * (1 - p)) / (e**2)

          # Adjusted sample size for finite population correction
          n_adjusted = n / (1 + ((n - 1) / N))

          n, n_adjusted
Out[17]:  (384.1599999999999, 382.69367093046276)
```

Figure 5: Sample Size Formula for Population of 100,000

Confidence Level	Z-Score	n	n (Adjusted)
95%	1.96	384.16	382.69
99%	2.576	663.50	659.13
99.99%	3.890	1,511.89	1,495.43

Table 8: Sample size for higher confidence level and 5% error margin

Feel free to calculate the sample size for 1 million patient records (population) with a 99.99% confidence level and 2% margin of error.

Improvising testing capabilities with each test iteration of data migration should be the logical way to progress and gradually improve the data migration success ratio with each test iteration. Data unit and data integrity testing should be part of all iterations to ensure that only clean and integrated data makes it into the target system. You can initiate functional testing when you load sufficient data into the target system hosted in a test environment with UI and authorized users/testers who could compare migrated data in the new system with their legacy avatar.

For example, you can begin comparing patient registration and update screens in the target system with the migrated data after a majority of legacy patient information, such as demographics data with their aliases, addresses, and next of kin, are migrated into the target system, whereas ppointment, waitlist, or any transactional data is yet to migrate. Let's say you could migrate 30,000 patients out of 100,000 in the last iteration, and a testing environment with migrated data is available with the UI. Then, at least 240 to 245 random patients (with $p = 0.2$) will be tested to determine the data migration process and identify areas of improvement in the next iteration.

Despite initially having a small amount of legacy data suitable for end-to-end migration during the early test iterations, incorporating functional testing in each iteration from the beginning will help maximize the testing scope, eliminate most issues before cutover, and build confidence in the data migration processes and ETL (Extract, Transform, Load) code. As you progress through multiple iterations of functional testing, expanding the scope incrementally with each cycle, it is essential to conduct a thorough final round of testing before the final cutover, when all required data has been migrated. This final round should be based on an optimal sample size calculated to confirm the successful completion of the data migration testing process.

The objectives of functional testing are:

- Test legacy data in the new system, checking that all transactional data is visible and behaves as intended in real scenarios.

- Conduct user acceptance testing (UAT) with sample data from real users to confirm the system performs as expected in daily operations.

- Ensure that the migration process has not altered or lost any data by comparing migrated data in the legacy system and the new system side by side.

- System Integration Testing (SIT) to check the end-to-end data flow, ensuring that upstream and downstream systems are integrated seamlessly.

Testing data migration is not a one-time activity. It's iterative and linked to iteration goals until no issues are found for multiple consecutive test iterations before the go-live. After one iteration, errors and failures that surfaced during the functional testing should move into the data integrity audits to prevent error-bound data from entering the target system. Many errors found during data integrity audits can move to data unit testing as business or data quality rules to be validated, and the data that violates the rule would be rejected from data transformation in the next test iteration.

Questions to Ask

By breaking down data migration testing into data unit, data integrity, and functional tests, you can ensure the accuracy, reliability, and performance of your migrated data. Each testing type helps you address potential issues before they impact your new system and business continuity. Ensuring all testing is iterative and integrated into your migration plan will lead to a smoother transition with fewer surprises at go-live.

This component addresses the following questions from stakeholders:

- How do we ensure data is migrated to the right place?

- How do we conduct data migration testing?

- How can we ensure that legacy data will migrate correctly with no scope for any loss of data or its transactional integrity?

- How can we ensure that migrated legacy data will not cause functional issues in the new business application?

- How can open transactions migrated from the legacy system be closed successfully in the target system?

- Can we compare legacy and new systems with real migrated data?

- How many records should we test to ensure confidence in a data migration?

- Can we integrate data migration testing with system integration and user-accepting testing?

CHAPTER 10

The Go-Live

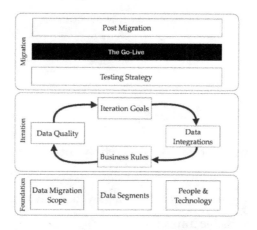

---

*The judgment day is all about your past
practices.*

It's the big day—brace yourself! You have done everything you
could using the data migration framework described in this book.
You have set the foundation right and done many iterations with

robust testing to eliminate all possible issues and risks. Go-live is your judgment day, where the cutover from the legacy system to the new world takes place, hopefully leading to a better system and a brighter future.

In data migration, the go-live day is the culmination of all your efforts. It's the day when everything you've meticulously planned and executed comes to fruition. However, with all the excellent planning, the go-live day is not just about flipping a switch. The go-live process needs meticulous planning and a series of steps to switch off a significant legacy business system that has been operational for over one or more decades and subsequently switch on the new system for the next few decades.

The Most Critical Step

The go-live process is a carefully orchestrated and well-coordinated sequence of actions, first to decommission the legacy business system and then to deploy the new system with the minimum possible impact on business continuity. Data migration is a mandatory cutover activity in the target system's deployment checklist on the go-live day. A Deployment Checklist is a comprehensive list of all the activities necessary to deploy a system or application to its target environment. Cutover activities are part of the broader deployment checklist that initiates the transition from the old system. These cutover activities include shutting down the old system, its integrations, and migrating data.

To ensure the highest data integrity, execute data migration after ensuring no user can log into the legacy system, all integrations are disabled, and no insert, update, or delete operations are possible on the legacy database. On the other hand, once data is migrated, you can only declare it a success once the target system is switched on with the migrated data and a smoke test is conducted in the new system to ensure things are working as expected.

Smoke test means you smell around and ensure nothing is burning after you turn on the lights of the new system with its maximum max pro features for your business.

Surprises in data migration activity on the go-live day can cause significant delays. The value proposition of the data migration framework described in this book is all about ensuring no surprises on the go-live day. Following the foundation and iteration components of the data migration framework will equip you as a project manager with confidence in your data migration processes for the big day, precise timeline, and resources needed to execute end-to-end data migration on the go-live day.

The Deployment RACI Checklist

Data migration activity has a lot of pre- and post-requisite activities that make it a success. Therefore, to manage the go-live day effectively, having a RACI matrix (Responsible, Accountable, Consulted, and Informed) [29] with each activity listed is highly desirable. You can choose your preferred alternatives to RACI as you wish, and start preparing the matrix well in advance before the go-live to ensure stakeholders know their roles and responsibilities. This preparation ensures that all key personnel are available and ready when needed to prevent any interruptions on the big day. The Deployment checklist can vary depending on the various factors. However, you can categories all deployment activities into the following groups:

- **Backup the Legacy System.** Start by taking a full backup of the legacy system, including the database and application. This acts as a safety net in case of any unexpected issues.

- **Disable System Integration.** Turn off all upstream and downstream integrations in the legacy system to stop any data flow during migration. This step is critical for ensuring data integrity.

- **Prepare Network and Infrastructure.** Adjust your network settings and infrastructure to support the new system. This may include updating firewalls, changing routes, and verifying sufficient bandwidth.

- **Execute Data Migration.** Move the data from the legacy system to the new system according to the defined migration plan. Precision is key during this phase, and following the framework can help.

- **Perform Smoke Testing.** Run basic tests on the new system to confirm that essential functionalities are working properly and that no critical issues exist.

- **Finalize Infrastructure Setup.** Ensure the new system's network and infrastructure configurations are completed and ready for operation.

- **Activate the New System.** Power up the new system, verify it's operational, and prepare for go-live.

- **Re-enable Integrations.** Restore upstream and downstream integrations to allow data flow between the new system and connected applications.

Several Checkpoints—Go or No-Go

Ensure everything is on track as planned. For a significant legacy system with multiple decades in production and several downstream dependencies, compiling a list of steps in each category above with RACI will quickly lead to an extensive checklist in an Excel file to run through on the go-live day with the support from internal (IT, architects, and engineers) and external (vendors) team members. Therefore, with many variables around, one should be ready for surprises on the big day and have clear criteria to denote the success or failure of each activity and the group as a whole. For example, a legacy business application may have multiple downstream integrations, and one integration may fail to switch off and unhook from the legacy system, or it failed to switch on with the new system after several attempts. Mind the fact that you are passing through downtime and do not have days or weeks to investigate issues that magically appear on the go-live night. Every minute matters during this phase.

In case of surprises or partial success of any step, the deployment checklist activity should include some time (20 to 30 minutes) as a contingency to investigate any issue or doubts in executing the activity in the deployment checklist. I remember waiting for my turn in a giant deployment checklist on my first data migration go-live day and then stealing the show for the next few hours. After every step, we had a clear and straightforward flag, "Go" or "No-Go," to indicate the current status and whether the checklist's next step should be executed. Therefore, follow the practice of Go or No-Go flags in your deployment checklist for the go-live day and add sufficient checkpoints and time to quadruple-check everything before moving to the next step.

In the case of a No-Go call during the transition, you should have a clear rollback plan based on the current transition stage. Think about what would happen if things went south in category number "6. Finalize Infrastructure Setup" on the go-live day. What would be the sufficient contingency time allocation for the people responsible to investigate and fix issues before a whole bunch of people can call it a day waiting for their turn and eventually keep a critical business application offline for business transactions? Therefore, accommodate clear communication with Go and No-Go calls for all stakeholders in the deployment checklist RACI, coupled with several thought-through checkpoints that give you breathing space to assess the progress and decide whether to proceed to the next step or halt.

Questions to Ask

The key to a successful go-live is meticulous planning, collaboration, and execution. The cutover day is the ultimate test of your implementation of the data migration framework described in this book. It's the day when all your planning, testing, and iterations come together. If you have followed the foundation and iteration component of the framework with a robust testing strategy, you will feel prepared and ready to hit the ground running on the go-live day.

By preparing and following a deployment checklist with RACI and ensuring thorough preparation, you can transition smoothly from the legacy system to a new, better world if you have answers for the following:

- What is the correct sequence for decommissioning the legacy system?

- Which resources must be available throughout the decommissioning process, and who do we need for specific tasks?

- What should be the criteria for rolling back the decommissioning?

- What should be the criteria for successfully decommissioning and shifting operations to the new system?

- After which point is rollback not possible?

- How many hours of downtime are required for the decommissioning?

- Can business processes remain on halt during downtime? If not, who will be responsible for the paper-based process and backfilling data in the new system after it goes live?

CHAPTER 11

Post Migration

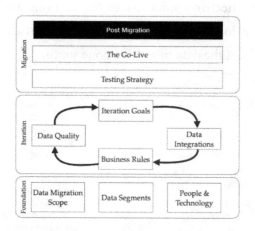

After all the excellent work for over a year or two, you will eventually execute the cutover. But guess what? You are not done yet, and it's too soon to call it a success. First of all, things could go south on the big day. Thus, the practical advice is to be ready for surprises and have robust contingency and rollback plans to control the anxiety (and excitement).

In 2018, TSB Bank attempted to migrate 5 million customer accounts to a new IT platform. Everything appeared smooth during testing, but post-migration monitoring was ignored. Once the system went live, thousands of customers lost access to their accounts, some saw incorrect balances, and unauthorized transactions appeared. The migration had data integrity issues, but no real-time monitoring was in place to detect and correct them. The CEO had to resign as a fallout, TSB suffered $330 million in losses, and trust in the bank collapsed [30]. This is the perfect example of why post-migration monitoring is not a luxury—it's a necessity. Sandesh Gawande, CEO and Founder of iceDQ, has effectively summarized the data migration disaster at TSB [31]. Below is a snippet from Sandesh's article highlighting the facts about the data migration gone south.

Cost / People	Category	Party	Description	Source
£318,000,000	Direct Migration Cost	TSB	Money spent on the actual migration project itself.	The Register
£247,000,000	Remediation Cost	TSB	Following the disastrous migration, TSB incurred additional costs for customer compensation, technical fixes, and increased staffing for customer service.	The Mirror
£48,650,000	Regulatory Fines	TSB	Fines paid by TSB Bank to FCA and PRA.	Reuters

Cost / People	Category	Party	Description	Source
£81,620	Regulatory Fines	Former CIO	The Prudential Regulation Authority (PRA) has fined the former Chief Information Officer (CIO) of TSB Bank plc (TSB).	Bank of England
£1,900,000	Customers unable to view their accounts	Customers	Customers didn't have access to their accounts. Overseas ATM withdrawals declined. Digital banking was completely stopped. Many unauthorized transactions were suspected.	BBC
£1,300	Customers money stolen	Customers	Money stolen from their accounts – in some cases their life savings – by fraudsters exploiting the bank's recent IT meltdown.	The Guardian

Table 9: Data Migration Gone South

Unlike TSB, those with the phased migration and subsequent planned cutovers will undergo one more iteration stage. New business rules will be required to manage partial business operations running on the new system from a specific date and time. Business units or areas parked for the next cutover may disclose never-before-seen data quality issues or new integration dependencies. You would have one more opportunity to learn from the last experience and avoid making the same mistakes while defining Iteration Goals for the next cutover. However, be it phased or a big bang, in this chapter, I concisely cover key activities post-data migration, which are mostly applicable to both.

Active Monitoring

If everything goes smoothly and as per the go-live run sheet, you still need to be vigilant and operate the target system under the hyper-care mode for the next 24 to 72 hours with the right people readily available to support, escalate, and resolve any functional issues. Smooth data migration during the cutover is the primary success of the people behind data migration. However, I would at least wait a week from the cutover to call data migration successful, given no adverse situation has arisen in the target system, downstream integrations, or business processes due to any data migration glitches. I want to include Lars Kjaersgaard's checklist for data migration [32] to highlight key activities for continuous monitoring post-migration:

- Establish ongoing monitoring processes to keep tabs on the performance and functionality of your newly migrated data.

- Set up alerts for critical errors, ensuring immediate attention when needed.

- Monitor key metrics like system downtime, data accuracy, and user feedback to spot potential issues.

- Swiftly address any problems or glitches, actively seeking ways to optimize performance.

Data Archival

Post-data migration, legacy data archival, and purging are critical areas to address. With data archival tasks parked after the successful data migration and legacy decommissioning, the objective is to ensure the data retention policies and guidelines are adhered to. You must ensure that whatever legacy data we need is available and accessible in the new system while unnecessary data is purged. Necessary historical data within the data retention needs can be made available in the new system with two possible methods:

1. Develop on-demand data migration to extract and transform particular subsets of legacy data when required in the new system.

2. Migrate all required historical data into the new system.

The first method would require access to legacy data in the source database or some data extracts form (CSV dumps) if access to the proprietary legacy database is gone with decommissioning. Out of the scope of this book, implementing this solution is a project on its own, with substantial efforts to build and manage such a solution. The second method can be a practical choice for many organizations, switching off the legacy system and accessing its data forever.

When choosing the second method to avail the historical data in the new system, a data migration process can be split into two parts:, active and inactive (or open and closed), to denote current and past transactions. Migrating only active data for current business transactions on the cutover day can minimize the decommissioning downtime by avoiding large volumes of legacy data for inactive transactions, which your users would not immediately need in the target system. In such cases, ensuring successful migration of required historical data after the cutover is essential before the legacy system can retire in peace for good.

Backfill Paper Trails

The show must go on for many businesses, including healthcare. You can't turn down a patient in an emergency because you are updating your patient management system. In such cases, paper-based processes are implemented as temporary measures to keep the lights on for business-as-usual during the system downtime. If you are in such 24x7 business operations, carefully plan your processes on paper for downtime and ensure the right timing for manually loading paper trails back into the new business applications once it is live.

Supporting Business Users

People habitually familiar with the blue screen UI, subconscious keyboard mastery, and applying brute force on the Enter key will need your support with the futuristic mouse-based UI in front of them to figure out where and how legacy data is migrated on which screens under what menu. You can coordinate with trainers or super users (admins) of the target system to support users with data-migration-related enquiries. I recommend bundling some knowledge base or documentation for frequently asked questions.

You must also support other business stakeholders with data analysis and report writing needs alongside new application users. From ad hoc analysis to producing operational reports, expect questions and inquiries from your data and analytics tribe, with similar questions on where and how legacy data is migrated to which schema and what tables. Note that having an endorsed data migration plan with reference to approved business rules will assist in promptly supporting both types of user inquiries.

You have moved to point B from point A successfully. Now, manage the jet lag well to regain your routine life.

Questions to Ask

Leverage the last component of the framework to set up clear SLAs for post-migration support, identify key resources for the downtime and hyper-care periods, and define criteria to infer data migration as a success. This component addresses the following questions from stakeholders:

- When and how can we confirm data migration success after the decommissioning?

- Can we park migrating any non-essential data after the cutover to reduce the downtime?

- Shall we train the trainers on the impacts of data migration on the target system UI and workflow?

- Can we move to a paper-based process during downtime?

- How do we ensure paper-based trails from downtime are entered back into the new system?

- How do we enable easy and prompt access to business rules of data migration to support business users in their BAU duties?

CHAPTER 12

The Larger Picture

Change is the only constant in the universe.

The day will surely come when you have to change your legacy business systems handling the core of your business. Mind that you don't get rid of the dinosaur for cheap. Retiring the legacy system and implementing enterprise-grade ERPs, CRMs, and similar administrative business applications are typically part of a larger digital transformation with a huge investment that easily ranges in millions. I have seen one with a 40-million-dollar budget and read about many such digital transformations costing much more for large enterprises in the public and private sectors.

Although the expense of replacing legacy systems is high, organizations must also consider technical debt, security vulnerabilities, and the limitations these outdated systems impose on innovation and efficiency, resulting in hidden costs greater than replacing legacy systems [33]. In my research on the negative impact of the legacy system on the business, I came across a compilation of 300 case studies of digital transformation [34], each describing the loss of business and below-average customer experience that forced organizations to digital transformation. I bet you may find a case study for your industry here: https://tinyurl.com/3w6d5fpy.

Opportunity – The Tech-Debt Remover Project

Such enterprise-level digital transformation is a once-in-a-decade or two (or three) event that brings the opportunity to make things better for your employees (or nurses) and give a good experience for your customers (or patients). If you are a manager for data migration, you have already covered all the necessary information that could guide you in managing the transition safely. However, on the leadership front, with several touchpoints in terms of integrations and business units, retiring legacy systems offers an opportunity to expand the scope of digital transformation and change management to optimize or discard old culture and habits around the data usage in your organization.

If you are in a leadership position who can see and influence the larger picture, you can instill a vision that drives the change toward a better world, and strategically leverage this decommissioning opportunity to initiate a change in the culture to make it truly **data-driven** that treats **data as an asset** and embraces **data governance**. Let's simplify this jargon below.

Data as an Asset

"Data is a business asset" is a widely used and accepted jargon frequently thrown in the open air because most of us subconsciously agree that the data produced by business operations can add value back to the business. Although the data holds the perception of value like other business assets, the distinct properties of data as an asset described below obfuscate the monetary value of the data in the daily business-as-usual operations. The monetary value of classic assets can be derived easily as the delta between the cost of an item and the benefit derived through that item [35]. On the other hand, the monetary valuation of data in business-as-usual is a complex task without any standards to define the cost of business data and its benefits.

This deficit of monetary valuation turns into the genesis of enterprise data mismanagement with symptoms such as no clear ownership of business data, no inventory of data assets, no proactive risk analysis of data misuse/loss, no data quality standards, etc. Therefore, reactive organizations with low data maturity (Mediocre and Losers) are subject to the sudden awakening of the monetary value of the data as an asset retrospectively when the business data is misused or lost already.

Data like tangible business assets

You put checks and balances in place to prevent loss or misuse of data, as you do for protecting physical or financial assets. Loss or misuse of physical or financial assets can result in monetary and reputational repercussions, as do the loss or misuse of a business' data assets.

Data unlike tangible business assets

Unlike physical assets, which can be physically touched and moved and are restricted to one location at a time, and financial assets, which require inclusion on a balance sheet, data possesses unique characteristics. It lacks tangibility, yet it boasts durability, maintaining its integrity over time even as its value may fluctuate [36]. Data is easily replicated and transferred, but restoration in the event of loss or damage can prove challenging or impossible in the worst case. Remarkably, data remains unconsumed during usage and can serve multiple individuals simultaneously, a feat unattainable with physical or financial assets [37].

Furthermore, the utilization of data often generates more data. For example, your annual report from your business data eventually becomes the archived business data. If leveraged and managed as a business asset, an organization with a data-driven culture can yield outstanding results in reducing IT infrastructure costs, optimizing business processes, packaging new products or services, and delivering a tangible ROI.

Data Driven Culture

Before we look at what is truly a data-driven organization, it would help to first realize the following factors that prevent an organization from becoming one:

- **Silos of systems with growth.** An organization onboards various business systems in its lifetime to meet the needs of different business units such as sales, marketing, operations, HR, etc. Each system is rolled out at different timespan with varying priorities and objectives, creating a web of business data captured and stored in various silos under different ownerships among business units (departments). Business units prefer to hire or consult data and BI experts internally to meet their business unit's reporting and analytical needs rather than liaising/pushing for an enterprise-wide data strategy. A business unit proposing a larger picture for enterprise data management must cross many loops and hops of the management hierarchy, data privacy and security, master data issues, etc., which eventually kills the momentum of the work stream and results in no outcome. Therefore, one business unit cannot propagate the data-driven culture in the entire organization.

- **Heavy IT operational cost.** It is common to find legacy systems running the core of business operations for over a decade or two in large organizations. Such legacy systems can have limitations regarding data procurement for analysis and downstream integration, with huge vendor dependency and relative costs for enhancing or modifying anything in legacy systems to meet data-driven objectives. Technology made initially to empower an organization becomes a growth hurdle and enslaves the organization, negating the scope for optimization, innovation, and ideas. Secondly, stakeholders see replacing or enhancing such legacy systems at the core of business operations as a considerable risk. "If something is running okay, let it run, don't touch it" syndrome from IT support can also discourage stakeholders from wanting to be data-driven due to uncertainties of business ownership and Return on Investment (ROI).

- **Cost of integrations**. Being data-driven involves integrating datasets from multiple business systems to produce coherent business data. This daunting task could involve numerous business units and management hierarchies collaborating. Variations in reference data (customer types, product segments) in different business systems and their poor data quality make integration more challenging and leave the business with limited descriptive analytics (what happened in the past).

- **Delays in Decision Making**. The above three factors eventually affect the semi- and non-technical decision makers with limited data literacy to be decisive about the business data and undertaking data-driven initiatives.

Data-driven is first about the culture's swiftness, which requires well-planned change management activities. The vagueness of risks and costs associated with data-driven initiatives coupled with different priorities of business units keep delaying decisions on crafting enterprise-level data strategy, data governance, and subsequent data initiatives.

Data-Driven Characteristics

One could simplify being data-driven by getting reliable, timely data to make prompt decisions. However, as always, the devil is in the details. Below is my endeavor to concisely define the key characteristics of a data-driven culture. Note that the first sign of being data-driven is the consensus at the executive (top-management) level on managing data professionally via the collaboration between the organization's technical and business leadership. If you can overcome the anti-factors described above, you can aim to gradually achieve the following key characteristics of a data-driven culture.

Applied Data Governance:

- Treating data like a business asset with lifecycle management.
- A foundation is set to control the habits, processes, and operations around the generation, storage, and usage and integration of data.

Low Data Latency:

Make it easy for employees (analysts) to promptly acquire the required data and intelligence with confidence and without violating any compliance.

- A mature eco-system encouraging self-service BI.

High Data Literacy:

- Common data vocabulary with business glossary.

The business is placed on the analytics continuum [38]:

Descriptive -> Predictive -> Prescriptive

- **Descriptive analytics** involves collecting and organizing historical data to present it in an easily understandable format. It uses basic mathematical and statistical tools to summarize past events without making predictions, serving as a foundation for further analysis. Visual tools such as line graphs and bar charts make the findings accessible to a broad business audience. Examples of descriptive analytics include summarizing past events such as sales or marketing campaigns, collating survey results, and reporting general trends.

- **Predictive analytics** uses historical data to forecast future outcomes by identifying patterns and trends. It employs techniques such as data mining, statistical modeling, and machine learning algorithms to make predictions based on probabilities. Deep learning, a subset of machine learning, mimics human neural networks to enhance prediction accuracy, with applications in areas like credit scoring and medical image analysis. Examples of predictive analytics include inventory forecasting, fraud detection and prevention, and predicting customer preferences to recommend products.

- **Prescriptive analytics** goes beyond describing and predicting by recommending the best actions to take. It uses advanced statistical and machine learning techniques to analyze both internal and external data, anticipating various future scenarios. Common applications of prescriptive analytics include GPS technology that recommends the best routes, predictive maintenance for optimizing equipment management, and identifying the best testing and patient groups for clinical trials.

Data Governance

Data migration is a data management task. However, existing data governance practices in your organization can add immense value in ensuring successful data migration initiatives. Data governance is about governing the management of data. In corporate governance, you govern the management of a corporation. Now, scale this definition. X-Governance is about oversight and control of actions on the X; management is about taking actual actions on the X. Good governance of X instills trust in people about X who are directly and indirectly impacted by or concerned about the management of X. Repeat this definition replacing X with Data, Corporate, and Nation.

Organizations serious about managing their data strategically would invest in a formal data governance program to prevent the data from being managed arbitrarily and subject to monetary and reputation loss. A data governance program is initiated to meet one of the following two objectives or a balanced mixture of both:

- **Data Conformance**. To comply with regulations and adherence to policies.
- **Data Performance**. To confidently leverage the business data for critical business decisions.

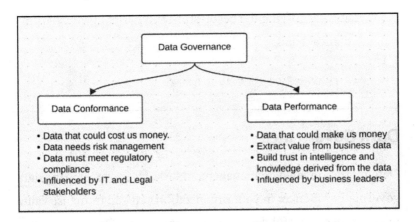

Figure 6: Data Governance Objectives

Data governance programs focused primarily on data performance are often referred to as "Data Enablement" to eliminate the negative perceptions associated with the term governance. Existing data governance (or data enablement) practices can directly support data migration efforts—from establishing data quality standards and business rules to accelerating data discovery and refactoring data warehouses, reporting structures, and other downstream integrations. On the flip side, data migration can also expose gaps in data governance.

For organizations with lower data management maturity and no formal data governance, legacy data migration presents an opportunity to review and streamline data utility needs while implementing the right controls to ensure compliance with regulations and policies—this is the **Data Conformance** aspect of data governance. As part of data migration, you may be able to identify laws and regulations affecting legacy data through publicly available information. However, finding universally endorsed and consistently enforced internal data policies may be far more challenging.

Ultimately, the extent to which you incorporate data governance into your migration effort depends on feasibility, desirability, and budget viability, along with your organization's appetite for change. You can proactively involve key stakeholders to define and enforce data policies as part of migration. Alternatively, a less aggressive approach is to leverage the gaps identified and controls applied during migration to build a business case for implementing data policies as part of a larger digital transformation initiative.

Before pursuing a like-for-like replacement of existing reports and data models from your current data warehouse, vaults, or marts, take a step back and assess the various types of data utilities your organization relies on. These can typically be grouped into three broad categories: **Operational Reporting, Management Reporting, and Analytics (including ML/AI).** Rationalizing your data utilities during the migration process may reveal that a significant portion of existing operational reports—and a fair share of management reporting—can be managed natively by the new system's out-of-the-box capabilities.

With a clearer understanding of compliance and regulatory requirements gained through the migration project, you may also identify unnecessary data movements or unintended exposure of personal information within reporting and data integration solutions. It is crucial to ensure that policies defined on paper are codified as enforceable rules within reporting and integration layers.

On the **Data Performance** side, or rather the lack of it, data migration projects often face delays due to challenges in legacy data discovery and ambiguity in business terminology. For instance, terms like **Length of Stay (LOS) for a patient** or **Revenue vs. Turnover** may be interpreted differently across business units. These variations can create confusion in defining scope, business rules, integrations, and data quality components within the migration framework. Such gaps highlight the need to invest in **enterprise business glossaries and data catalog solutions** to enhance data performance through governance practices. Business glossaries serve as a repository for policy definitions and intent, while data catalogs provide enriched metadata interfaces that indicate which policies and data quality standards are applied to datasets, and individual attribute/field of a table.

Question to Ask

Having a data-driven culture that treats data as an asset with formal data governance is a dream place to be when planning for legacy retirement. However, if your data management maturity is low, use your legacy decommissioning project as a "Tech-Debt Remover" initiative. This approach will help you take a strategic leap forward while addressing the barriers preventing a true data-driven culture. Seize this golden opportunity to enhance overall data management practices and establish strong data hygiene—ensuring that once the new system is operational, data remains clean, consistent, and well-governed.

- Can we leverage this opportunity to change our shoddy data usage habits and be strategic about data management?

What's Next for Data Migration?

The world of enterprise IT is shifting rapidly. With the rise of AI-driven data transformation, low-code/no-code migration platforms, and increasing regulatory scrutiny, data migration is no longer just about moving records from Point A to Point B. The next decade will see:

- **AI-Powered Data Mapping.** Tools that automatically detect mapping inconsistencies.
- **Self-Healing Migration Pipelines.** Automated rollback for failed migrations.
- **Regulatory-First Data Migrations.** Compliance-driven migrations with real-time audibility.

> *If you take away one key message from this book, let it be this: a data migration is never just a technical exercise—it's a business transformation. Treat it as such.*

CHAPTER 13

The Question Set

Each chapter above ends with a series of questions to be addressed by stakeholders, and the answers should be reflected in the data migration plan within the component of the data migration framework described in that chapter. All questions across all components of the framework are listed here and grouped into three segments.

- **Foundation** components of the framework will assist you in discovery and scope refinement.

- **Iteration** components of the framework focus solely on the nuances of executing test-runs of data migration and making the most out of it.

- **Migration** components cover the critical stage of executing the switchover with control and confidence.

Foundation - Data Migration Scope

- Can we quantify the volume of data to be migrated to the new system, and what is the reasoning behind this volume?

- Is there a single legacy system or multiple instances at different locations?

- Should we migrate all data across the enterprise in one go or take a cautious, phased approach with multiple small migrations?

- What are the pros and cons of the big-bang and phased approach?

- If multiple instances of the legacy system are running, what would be the most logical order for decommissioning them?

- What would happen to the data outside the scope, and what if we need the out-of-scope historical data in the future while it is not available in the new business system?

- What information about the legacy system's data structures is available via system documentation or data dictionaries?

- What is the status of in-house or vendor-based technical support for data archival and purging?

Foundation - Data Segments

- Can we identify and differentiate business data in the migration scope into logical segments, such as master and transaction data?

- When can we start data migration activities during the decommissioning project's life cycle?

- What legacy data is low-hanging fruits that can be migrated in the first test run?

- Do we have alternative data sources, such as a data warehouse or another business system, for the master data within the scope of migration?

- Is complete data migration offered as a managed service by the vendor of the target system?

- Shall we wait for the data migration testing until all data is entirely migrated to the new application, or shall we start the data migration testing in phases early on?

- What types of regulatory and policy compliances are applied to the legacy data within the migration scope?

- How do we ensure the data migration test runs do not violate data compliance?

- Can we ethically use real data without privacy violations for the data migration testing with screen-to-screen comparisons?

Foundation - People and Technology

- Which specific tools and personnel are essential for executing a successful data migration?

- Does the vendor provide managed services for data migration?

- Can we use our current Extract, Transform, and Load (ETL) solution and resources for the data discovery and transformation processes, considering the potential cost and time savings?

- Which toolset should we choose for ETL, such as SSIS, Informatica, Python, etc?

- Shall we host the data migration solution on-premises or in the cloud?

- What are the licensing cost and consulting costs for data migration tools?

- When was the last time a data management maturity assessment was done, and what was the outcome?

- As a part of project preparation, shall we undertake a professional data management maturity assessment?

- Have we evaluated the availability and skillsets of SMEs and technical team members to support data migration?

- Should we onboard specialist consultants and end-to-end data migration software to manage data migration professionally?

- What is the risk and possible impact due to limited in-house resource availability for data migration?

- How could we ensure that all information/metadata generated during data migration, such as decisions made and business rules defined, is captured for future reference?

Iteration - Business Rules
- Are we migrating all critical data elements in the legacy system into the new system for regulatory, financial, and operational needs?

- How are we handling mandatory data in the target system that is unavailable in the source system?

- What is the process for defining and validating mapping between source and target as business rules?

- What is the process for finding information about how we migrated legacy data after the decommissioning?

- What are the criteria to select the correct customer /product/ patient (master data) when duplicates are found within one legacy system or between multiple instances of the legacy systems?

Iteration - Data Quality

- What is the state of data quality in the legacy system, and what are the current data quality standards/practices?

- How do we measure the quality of legacy data to ensure it is fit for purpose, and who is responsible for the high quality of legacy data?

- Does the current state of data quality negatively impact the fitness of the legacy data for migration?

- Is this the opportunity to do things better in terms of monitoring data quality in the legacy system?

- How would we ensure that invalid data does not disrupt the new system or downstream integration for data warehousing and reporting?

- Which data quality enforcement/standards are implemented in the target system?

- Are data quality and integrity audits in place by the vendor before migrating legacy data into the new system?

- How should we measure data quality and form a roadmap for gradual improvements?

- How can manual and automated data cleansing efforts be efficiently planned?

Iteration - Data Integration

- Do we have a data warehouse for reporting with data feeds from the legacy system?

- Have we evaluated the impact of data migration on the existing data integrations?

- Have we gathered and evaluated downstream integration requirements?

- Do we have a list of must-haves, should, and could-have classifications of desired integration?

- How do we manage post-go-live continuity for operational and management reporting?

- How will we meet critical operational reporting required from day one post-go-live?

- Who should take risk ownership for uninterrupted data integration—the BAU data management team or the project team?

- What are the estimated refactoring efforts in terms of time and cost to upgrade data warehouse processes and data models to accept data from the new system?

Iteration - Iteration Goals

- How frequently are trial migrations scheduled before the cutover?

- Have we defined the measures to track data migration progress with each trial run?

- How do we identify showstoppers or blockers preventing successful data migration?

Migration - Testing Strategy

- How do we ensure data is migrated to the right place?

- How do we conduct data migration testing?

- How can we ensure that legacy data will migrate correctly with no scope for any loss of data or its transactional integrity?

- How can we ensure that migrated legacy data will not cause functional issues in the new business application?

- How can open transactions migrated from the legacy system be closed successfully in the target system?

- Can we compare legacy and new systems with real migrated data?

- How many records should we test to ensure confidence in a data migration?

- Can we integrate data migration testing with system integration and user-accepting testing?

Migration - The Go-Live

- What is the correct sequence for decommissioning the legacy system?

- Which resources must be available throughout the decommissioning process, and who do we need for specific tasks?

- What should be the criteria for rolling back the decommissioning?

- What should be the criteria for successfully decommissioning and shifting operations to the new system?

- After which point is rollback not possible?

- How many hours of downtime required for the decommissioning?

- Can the business process remain on halt during the downtime? If no, who is responsible for paper-based process and backfilling data in the new system after go-live?

Migration - Post Migration
- When and how can we confirm data migration success after the decommissioning?

- Can we park migrating any non-essential data after the cutover to reduce the downtime?

- Shall we train the trainers on the impacts of data migration on the target system UI and workflow?

- Can we move to a paper-based process during downtime?

- How do we ensure paper-based trails from downtime are entered back into the new system?

- How to enable easy and prompt access to business rules of data migration to support business users in their BAU duties?

The Larger Picture

- Can we leverage this opportunity to change our shoddy habits around data usage, and be strategic about data management?

About the Author

Krupesh Desai is a Certified Data Management Professional (CDMP) Associate, passionate about creating value by solving data-intensive problems. Currently serving as a Data Governance Technical Specialist, Krupesh brings over a decade of experience tackling complex data management challenges across various industries. He commenced as a software engineer working on database recovery and replication solutions, evolving into leadership and consulting roles in data migration, integration, and business intelligence.

Krupesh has successfully led multiple legacy decommissioning projects in the public health sector in New Zealand, delivering robust data migration, integration, and analytics solutions. As a BI Development Lead, Senior BI Consultant, and data architect, he has deployed cutting-edge tools and platforms for data warehousing automation, data visualization, and cloud data platforms to drive enterprise-wide transformation. Krupesh is a lifelong learner who believes in simplifying the language of data for decision makers. His research and writing focus on practical ways for effective data strategies.

Bibliography

Chapter 1

[1] Experian. (2017). *Data Migration Research Study*. Retrieved from https://www.experian.co.uk/assets/data-quality/data-migration-research-study-2017.pdf

[2] BridgeHead Software. (2022). *All You Need to Know About Legacy Application Retirement*. Retrieved from https://www.bridgeheadsoftware.com/2022/04/all-you-need-to-know-legacy-application-retirement/

[3] DAMA International. (2018). *Data Integration and Interoperability*. In *Data Management Body of Knowledge* (DMBOK) (2nd ed., pp. 292). Technics Publications.

Chapter 2

[4] Bisbal, J., Lawless, D., Wu, B., and Grimson, J. (1999). Legacy information system migration: A brief review of problems, solutions, and research issues. *Journal of Systems and Software*, 56(3), 231–242.

[5] Lynn, J. (n.d.). Core Principles for Application Decommissioning and Data Archiving. *Healthcare IT Today*. Retrieved from https://tinyurl.com/5xskensx

[6] Project Management Institute. (n.d.). *Qualitative risk assessment: Cheaper, faster and maybe better?* Retrieved March 31, 2025, from https://www.pmi.org/learning/library/qualitative-risk-assessment-cheaper-faster-3188

[7] Open Web Application Security Project (OWASP). (n.d.). *OWASP Risk Rating Methodology*. Retrieved March 31, 2025, from

https://owasp.org/www-community/OWASP_Risk_Rating_Methodology

Chapter 3

[8] DAMA International. (2018). *Data Integration and* Interoperability. In Data Management Body of Knowledge (DMBOK) (2nd ed., pp. 270–272). Technics Publications.

[9] Keller, W. (2000). The bridge to the new town: A legacy system migration pattern. In Proceedings of EuroPLoP 2000.

[10] Wagner, M., and Wellhausen, T. (2010). Patterns for data migration projects. In Proceedings of the 15th European Conference on Pattern Languages of Programs (EuroPLoP).

[11] Rüping, A. (2013). Transform! Patterns for data migration. In Noble, J., Johnson, R., Zdun, U., and Wallingford, E. (Eds.), Transactions on Pattern Languages of Programming III (Vol. 7840, pp. 1–36). Springer. https://doi.org/10.1007/978-3-642-38676-3_1

[12] Informatica. (n.d.). Master Data Management and Data Migration. Retrieved from https://tinyurl.com/2sawhmu8

[13] DAMA International. (2018). Data Security. In Data Management Body of Knowledge (DMBOK) (2nd ed., pp. 236–237). Technics Publications.

Chapter 4

[14] Temenos. (n.d.). *Hopp Temenos*. Retrieved November 10, 2024, from https://www.temenos.com/community/exchange/providers/hopp-temenos/

[15] DAMA International. (2018). *Data Management Maturity Assessment.* In *Data Management Body of Knowledge* (DMBOK) (2nd ed., pp. 531–549). Technics Publications.

[16] Data Strategy Pros. (n.d.). *Comparison of Data Management Maturity Assessments (DMMA).* Retrieved from https://www.datastrategypros.com/resources/data-management-maturity-assessment-dmma

Chapter 5

[17] DAMA International. (2018). *Data Integration and Interoperability.* In *Data Management Body of Knowledge* (DMBOK) (2nd ed., pp. 289). Technics Publications.

[18] Prasad, S. S. S. R. K., and Raju, K. V. S. N. (2021). Data migration need, strategy, challenges, methodology. *Open Journal of Business and Management,* 9(2), 350–362. https://doi.org/10.4236/ojbm.2021.92019

[19] Thalheim, B., and Wang, Q. (2013). Data migration: A theoretical perspective. *Data and Knowledge Engineering,* 87, 260–278. https://doi.org/10.1016/j.datak.2012.12.003

Chapter 6

[20] DAMA International. (2018). Data Quality. In Data Management Body of Knowledge (DMBOK) (2nd ed., pp. 473–477). Technics Publications.

[21] TechTarget. (n.d.). 6 dimensions of data quality boost data performance. Retrieved December 22, 2024, from

https://www.techtarget.com/searchdatamanagement/tip/6-dimensions-of-data-quality-boost-data-performance

[22] Precisely. (n.d.). Data quality dimensions: How do you measure up? Retrieved November 22, 2024, from https://www.precisely.com/blog/data-quality/data-quality-dimensions-measure

[23] Collibra. (n.d.). The 6 dimensions of data quality. Retrieved January 22, 2025, from https://collibra.com/us/en/blog/the-6-dimensions-of-data-quality

[24] Mago, S. (2024). SAP business transformation: Steps for effective cutover and data migration. *International Journal of Computer Trends and Technology*, 72(8), 224. https://doi.org/10.14445/22312803/IJCTT-V72I8P131

Chapter 7

[25] DAMA International. (2018). *Data Integration and Interoperability*. In Data Management Body of Knowledge (DMBOK) (2nd ed., pp. 269-270). Technics Publications.

[26] Bisbal, J., Lawless, D., Wu, B., and Grimson, J. (1999). Legacy information system migration: A brief review of problems, solutions, and research issues. *Journal of Systems and Software, 56*(3), 231–242. https://doi.org/10.1016/S0164-1212(99)90036-7

Chapter 8

[27] DAMA International. (2018). *Data Management and Organizational Change Management*. In *Data Management Body of Knowledge* (DMBOK) (2nd ed., pp. 582–586). Technics Publications.

Chapter 9

[28] Cochran, W. G. (1977). *Sampling techniques* (3rd ed.). John Wiley and Sons.

Chapter 10

[29] Atlassian. (n.d.). *RACI chart: What is it and how to use it.* Retrieved December 17, 2024, from https://www.atlassian.com/work-management/project-management/raci-chart

Chapter 11

[30] Slaughter and May. (2019). Independent review of TSB Bank's 2018 IT migration. TSB Bank. Retrieved February 2, 2025, from https://www.tsb.co.uk/news-releases/slaughter-and-may.html

[31] iCEDQ. (n.d.). TSB Bank data migration failure. Retrieved October 24, 2024, from https://icedq.com/resources/case-studies/tsb-bank-data-migration-failure

[32] Kjaersgaard, L. (2023, November 22). Step-by-Step Checklist for Successful Data Migration. Hopp Tech. Retrieved December 22, 2024 from https://hopp.tech/resources/data-migration-blog/checklist//

Chapter 12

[33] Incepta Solutions. (2024, August 15). *The hidden costs of legacy systems: Beyond financial burdens.* Retrieved October 22, 2024, from https://www2.inceptasolutions.com/the-hidden-costs-of-legacy-systems-beyond-financial-burdens

[34] Bridges, M. (2024, July 17). 300 case studies exploring digital transformation across various industries. Retrieved August 15, 2024,

from https://mark-bridges.medium.com/300-case-studies-exploring-digital-transformation-across-various-industries-30b2ad38bbab

[35] DAMA International. (2018). Data Management. In Data Management Body of Knowledge (DMBOK) (2nd ed., pp. 24). Technics Publications.

[36] Redman, T. (1996). Data Quality for the Information Age (pp. 41–42, 232–236).

[37] Data Driven (2008). Chapter 1—"The Wondrous and Perilous Properties of Data and Information."

[38] UNSW Online. (n.d.). Descriptive, predictive, and prescriptive analytics: What *are the differences?* Retrieved March 31, 2025, from https://studyonline.unsw.edu.au/blog/descriptive-predictive-prescriptive-analytics

Index

www.ingramcontent.com/pod-product-compliance
Lightning Source LLC
Chambersburg PA
CBHW071247050326
40690CB00011B/2297